Catrina

The Horse Illustrated Guide to

Caring *for* *Your* Horse

BY LESLEY WARD

The Horse Illustrated Guide to

Caring *for Your* Horse

BY LESLEY WARD

BOWTIE™
PRESS

A Division of Fancy Publications
Irvine, California

Ruth Berman, editor-in-chief
Nick Clemente, special consultant
Cover and book design copyright © 1998 by
Michele Lanci-Altomare

The horses in this book are referred to as *he* or *she* in alternating chapters unless their gender is apparent from the activity discussed.

Library of Congress Cataloging-in-Publication Data

Ward, Lesley.
    The horse illustrated guide to caring for your Horse / Lesley Ward.
        p.   cm.
    ISBN 1-889540-10-2 (alk. paper)
    1. Horses.   I. Title.
    SF285.3.W37   1998   98-20447
    636.1'083- -dc21   CIP

BowTie™ Press
3 Burroughs
Irvine, California 92618

Manufactured in the United States of America
First Printing September 1998
10 9 8 7 6 5 4 3 2 1

ACKNOWLEDGMENTS

I would like to thank the following people
for their help with this book:

Marian Abe; Sharon Biggs; Jane Butteriss; Marge Fritze;

Jane Frusher; Paula Grimstead; Sharon Biggs Hackney;

Diane Harkey; Moira Harris; Lon Hyers; Kelly James;

Denise Justice; Eric Matthews; Julie Mignery; Carol Nelson;

Jennifer Oltmann; Sherry Pascual; Heather Hayes Schram;

Jennifer Smith; Annette Slowinski, DVM; Katherine Waldrop;

and finally my father, Alan Ward, for his excellent editing skills.

CONTENTS

Introduction

You've finally found the horse of your dreams! He's passed the vet exam, you've paid for him, and you've taken him home. Now the fun truly begins! Your new horse is going to need a lot of your time, and it is up to you to keep him healthy and happy. The way he looks and feels largely depends on the way you care for him, so you'd better do it right!

This book describes the basics of horse care and management—important information that every horse owner needs to know. You'll learn how to handle your horse and make his new home a comfortable and safe place. You'll also learn about grooming, feeding, and tacking up. This book is full of tips to keep your horse healthy and in tip-top shape. You'll know if your horse isn't feeling 100 percent and what to do if he gets injured.

Owning a horse is a major responsibility. Even if your horse is kept at a boarding facility and others do most of the work for you, it's in your best interest to know as much as you can about horse health and stable management. Nobody truly cares about your horse as much as you do—or has your investment in his well-being. Even at the best barns, illnesses are missed and injuries are overlooked. You need to be familiar with your horse from head to hoof.

Taking care of a horse can sometimes be a lot of work, but the rewards are great. A horse who is properly cared for has a lot of energy and is fun to ride. If he eats the right diet and is groomed on a regular basis, he'll look great and you'll be proud of him—whether competing at a show or simply walking him around the barn. Looking after a living, breathing, occasionally unpredictable 1,000-plus-pound animal can be a challenge at times, but this book will prepare you for the task.

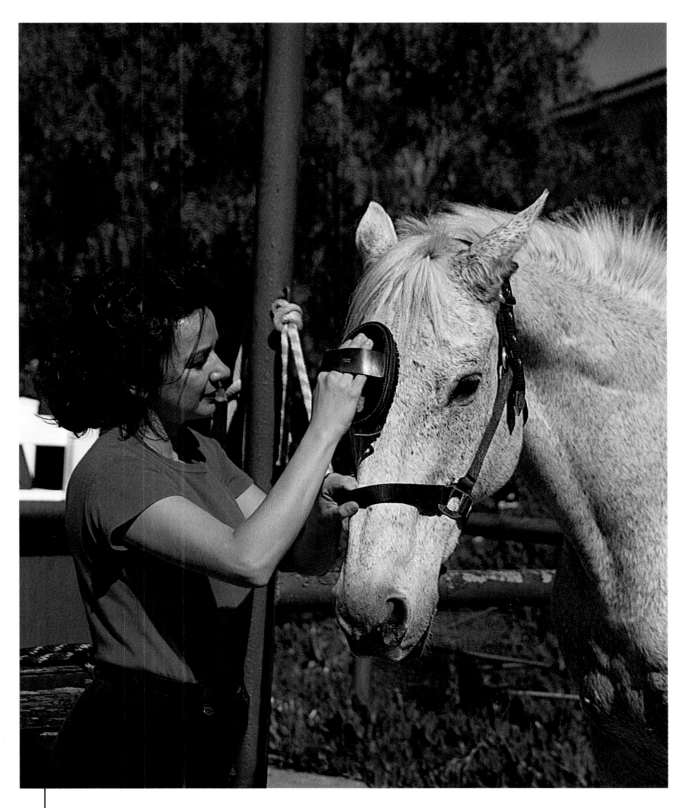

Taking care of a horse is time consuming,
but the rewards are many.

Handling a Horse

IF YOU'VE BEEN TAKING REGULAR RIDING LESSONS, you already have had some handling experience. Handling describes the activities you do with a horse while on the ground such as catching him, leading him, and working around him.

It's very important to learn correct handling for your own safety because safety should be your number one goal. Horses can be unpredictable, and even the quietest, most sensible horse can spook, break his lead rope, and run off.

Horses feel safer if they have company.

When a horse is upset, he will step on you or knock you over without a thought because his instinct is to escape whatever is upsetting him. This is why you should never relax around a horse. Almost anything could happen.

UNDERSTANDING HORSE BEHAVIOR

Understanding horse behavior helps you know how to react if your horse acts badly or does something that seems strange. Here are a few things to consider:

Horses, by nature, are herd creatures. They like to be in the company of other horses. This behavior dates back thousands of years to when your horse's ancestors lived in the wild. It was much safer for them to live in a herd because a solitary horse was more likely to get attacked and eaten by a predator. This is why some horses are hard to catch when out in a field. Similarly, if you are riding a horse in company, he may not want to leave his buddies.

Horses would rather run than fight. Running is their primary defense; this is why they spook or shy (jump or run away from a scary object) so much. If they spot something they think is dangerous, their natural reaction is to run away from it—a response that may have helped them survive for millions of years. Remember this when your horse reacts violently to a flapping garbage bag or an unusual noise. His first reaction may be to get away from it at top speed.

Horses take their cues from other horses. If one horse misbehaves, for example, in the warm-up arena at a show, it is likely that others will catch on and act badly too. If one horse won't be caught in a field, others may be difficult to catch too.

Horses have remarkable memories. This can be good and bad! A good memory is a plus when you teach a horse a new task and he remembers it the next time. But if he has a bad experience, such as a terrible ride in a trailer or a painful visit with the veterinarian, he will remember it for years.

HORSE SENSE

A horse can smell things you can't, hear things you can't, and see things you can't. That's why he may react strongly to something you don't sense. He may be nervous because he can smell a coyote a mile down the trail, or he may spook at a child running behind you in the arena. It's important to know about the senses that keep a horse aware of what's going on around him.

Vision

Horses see things clearly at a distance but have trouble keeping closer objects in focus. That's why a sack of feed three feet away can strike terror into the heart of a nervous horse. Horses have much better night vision than we do, and because a horse's eyes are set on the sides of his head, he has peripheral vision. He can see things on either side of him but not things directly ahead. He has several blind spots that you should know about when handling him. Move carefully around the following areas:

Directly behind the tail

Directly in front of the forehead

Under his head and around the front legs

If you have to groom a horse around these areas, speak to the horse so he knows where you are.

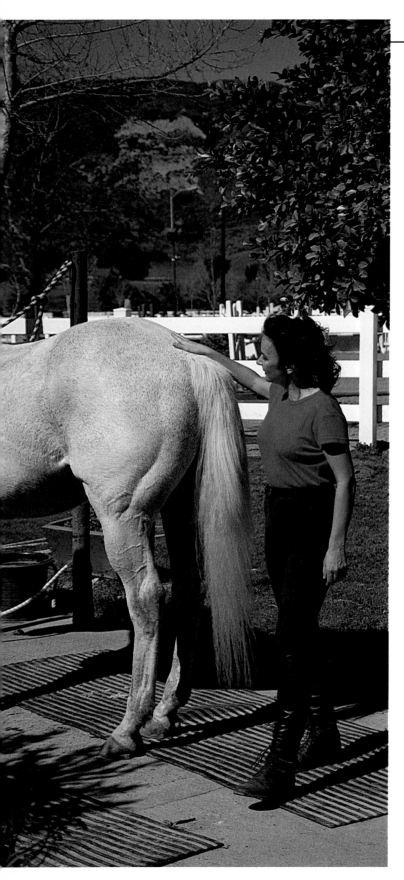

*Let a horse know when you
are behind him.*

Hearing

A horse has large, funnel-shaped ears that catch
even the tiniest noise. They also rotate so the
horse can hear sounds from any direction. If a
horse hears something that interests him, both of
his ears will point toward the source of the sound.

Smell

When a horse spots something scary, once he
feels brave enough he'll give it a big sniff. If he
meets a new horse, he'll sniff him, too, so that
later the other horse can be identified as familiar and safe, or hostile and dangerous. Your
horse will soon come to recognize your smell.

Touch

A horse's skin is very sensitive. Notice how he
can flick away the tiniest fly, no matter where it
lands on his body. Some horses hate being
groomed with a hard brush and fidget and grind
their teeth. Make your horse happy and use a
soft brush. The areas around the nose and
mouth are particularly sensitive, so avoid pat-
ting or touching him there. You might think
stroking your horse's nose would be soothing,
but he'd probably prefer that you pat him on the
neck instead.

Ears forward mean a horse is interested in something.

HORSE "TALK"

A horse's body language can tell you what he's feeling and help you predict what he's going to do. Accidents can be avoided if you pay close attention to your horse's body language.

Here are some interpretations of horse body language:

Pinning his ears back means he feels angry or threatened. Watch out—he may kick or bite!

Pawing with front hooves means he is impatient or hungry.

Swishing his tail violently means he is irritated or grumpy.

Swinging his hindquarters toward you means he's afraid of you or he may kick.

Lifting a leg could mean he is preparing to kick.

Ears forward, head reaching toward you means he's interested in you. He may be asking, "Hey, do you have a treat for me?"

Resting a hind leg could mean he is tired or simply feeling relaxed.

CATCHING A HORSE

If your horse spends most of his time in a field or corral, you'll have to catch him before you can ride him. This might be difficult because you should turn him out without a halter. Halters, especially tough nylon ones, can get caught on branches or a fence and seriously injure your horse. If your horse is hard to catch, turn him out in a leather halter—it will break if it gets caught on something.

If your horse is friendly, catching him shouldn't be difficult—especially if you have a tasty treat, such as an apple, in your pocket. Here's the best way to catch a horse:

1. Carry a halter and a lead rope into the field. Close the gate behind you. Call to your horse so he knows you're approaching. Walk slowly toward him. If he doesn't come, walk toward his side so he can see you clearly. Aim for his left shoulder so you'll be in the correct position to put on his halter quickly.

2. Stand on his near (left) side, next to his shoulder, and face the same direction he's facing. Give him a treat as a reward for coming to you or standing still, then slip the lead rope over his neck and hold the two parts of the rope together with one hand under his throat. This gives you some control so it is harder for your horse to escape.

3. Place the noseband of the halter over his nose, then pass the headpiece behind his ears, and buckle it. Always give him a pat on the neck to let him know how good he is. Being caught should be a pleasant experience!

Stand on the horse's near (left) side when catching him.

Catch Me if You Can!

Some horses don't like to be caught, and there are few things more annoying than chasing a wily horse around a field for hours! Here are some tricks that might help:

Many horses associate being caught with working. Go out in the field occasionally just to visit your horse. Put on his halter, give him a treat, and then let him go.

Carry the halter and lead rope behind your back so the horse can't see it.

Most horses are greedy and investigate anything that sounds like food. If your horse is by himself in the field, carry a bucket with some feed and shake it. Put down the bucket, and he should put his head in it. Wrap the lead rope around his neck and, *voilà*, he's trapped. Never carry a bucket of feed into a field full of horses; they may fight over it and you could get kicked.

Horses are nosy. Carry a squeaky toy or a crumpled piece of paper and squeak or rustle it near your horse. If he comes over, move slowly so as not to frighten him off.

Walk in a large circle around your horse, then slowly spiral in until you're close enough to put on his halter.

If you're desperate, lead his field mates out of the field. Your horse will probably loiter around the gate, eager to be with them. When he is alone, he may be easier to catch.

A bucket of food may entice a hard-to-catch horse.

TURNING OUT A HORSE

Open the gate wide enough for you and your horse to walk through side by side. Once you're in the field, turn your horse around so he is facing the gate. Close the gate, take off his halter, and let him go. Don't let your horse loose when he is facing the field. He might get frisky and try to run off, and you could get kicked.

Face the gate when turning out a horse.

LEADING A HORSE IN A HALTER

Stand next to your horse's shoulder, facing the same direction that he's facing. (He should be on your right.) Clip the lead rope to the metal ring on the halter under his chin. Your right hand should hold the lead rope about 3 inches under the chin. Loop the excess rope and hold it with your left hand. Don't wind it around your hand because if your horse runs off, you could be dragged behind him. Walk even to your horse's shoulder; don't get too far in front or behind.

To stop him, come to a complete halt and say "whoa." If he does not stop immediately, tug once or twice on the lead rope with your right hand and say "whoa" again.

Hold the lead rope with two hands.

A *"puller"* may require a chain over his nose.

LEADING PROBLEMS

If your horse likes to drag you along and nibble every blade of grass, you may have to use a chain over his nose to keep him under control. You can buy one at a tack store for a couple of dollars. Thread the snap end through the square bit of metal on the buckle (left) side of the halter, run it over the noseband, thread it through the square on the far side, and then snap it to the round ring halfway up his head. Then attach the lead rope to the chain at the bottom. Walk next to your horse normally, but if he tries to get away from you, tug on the lead rope. This pulls on the chain, which puts pressure on his nose. He should listen to you pretty quickly, and after a few days you should be able to remove the chain.

If your horse is sluggish when you lead him, carry a crop. A long, dressage-type crop is best because it reaches his hindquarters—the prime tapping area. Hold the lead rope as usual, and carry the crop in your left hand. If your horse does not move forward when you ask, flick the crop sideways behind you and tap him on his hindquarters so he understands that you want him to move—now!

TYING UP A HORSE

Always tie your horse in a safe place, with plenty of space between him and other horses. Always tie him in a halter. Never tie your horse with his reins because if he spooks, he will pull back, the bridle may break, and the bit will hurt his mouth.

Tie your horse to a specially mounted metal ring or a solid object such as a tree or fence post. Never tie him to anything that isn't firmly planted in the ground that he could run away with—such as a picnic table! As a safety precaution, tie a loop of safety string (usually baling twine) first and then tie the lead rope to the string. If your horse pulls back, he will break the string instead of his lead rope, his halter, or even his neck.

Tie him up high so he can't trip over the lead rope, and don't leave much slack in the rope. About 18 inches from the ring or post is adequate. And always keep an eye on your horse when he is tied up. It takes only a few seconds for a horse to get into trouble and hurt himself!

Always tie the lead rope to a loop of twine.

A quick-release knot is simple to learn. First, make a circle with the lead rope.

Make a loop with the excess rope and slip it through the first circle.

Tighten the circle by pulling on the section of rope that is closest to the lead snap and your horse's head.

QUICK-RELEASE KNOT

Always use a quick-release knot, which should come undone immediately with a strong tug on the free end. Here's how to tie one:

1. Thread the end of the lead rope through the loop made of safety string.

2. Form the loose end of the lead rope into a loop as shown.

3. Make another loop with the loose end and thread this under and through the first loop.

4. Leave the second loop hanging, then tighten the knot by pulling it and the rope attached to your horse at the same time.

5. To release the knot, pull on the loose end of the rope and it should come undone.

Chapter Two

YOUR HORSE'S HOME

BEFORE YOU BRING YOUR HORSE HOME, THINK about where she will live. Some horses live in fields, others live in stables. Many spend their days outdoors and come inside at night. Horses on the West Coast often live outside in small, sandy corrals. Where you live will probably determine her lifestyle.

When searching for a home for your horse, try to find a place with a field or turn-out area. A horse belongs outside as much as possible. Keeping a horse cooped up in a stable or tiny pen twenty-four hours a day is unnatural and can cause behavioral problems that stem from physical and mental distress. A horse is happiest with other horses and where she can move around, exercise herself, and nibble on grass. Spending part of every day outside adds variety to her life and helps her relax. Breathing fresh air and basking in sunshine keeps her healthy.

If your horse is a hardy mixed breed with the ability to grow a shaggy, warm coat, she may be happy to live outside all the time, even in a cold climate if given a lot of food and hay. But a thin-skinned, purebred horse, such as an Arabian or a Thoroughbred, has to be stabled at night in a cold area. This kind of horse may lose condition or become ill if kept outside all of the time.

THE FIELD-KEPT HORSE

If your horse is going to spend time in a field, it must be 100 percent safe. If there is only one hazard in a field, a horse is sure to find it, and it takes only a second or two for a horse to hurt herself, leaving you with a huge vet bill. Better to horse proof the field. Walk around the field and run a safety check of the following:

Fencing

A field must have a strong fence without gaps or broken parts. Most horse people agree that a wooden post-and-plank fence is the safest, but new, synthetic (plastic) fences are gaining in popularity. There are also new horse-friendly welded-wire fences, made of squares so small that your horse can't catch her foot in them. The fence should be at least 4 feet high; an athletic horse can jump over anything lower.

Some people use electric fencing, but by itself, it's not completely horse proof. A frightened horse may ignore the wire and gallop right through it. It is sometimes used as a "scare wire" on the inside of a fence—for extra protection—or occasionally to break up a bigger field so that grazing areas can be rotated. If you use electric fencing, tie colorful plastic strips to it. These

Natural Hazards

Walk around the field to make sure there are no holes. Fill in any holes you find with rocks and dirt. A hole can break a horse's leg. Put a fence around a huge hole.

Look for fruit-bearing trees. When the fruit ripens, pick it up before your horse gets it. Some horses get colic—a dangerous stomachache—after pigging out on ripening apples. Cherry tree leaves, red maple leaves, and oak tree acorns can be dangerous too. Finally, check for poisonous plants such as yew and hemlock and remove them. Many ornamental flowers and bushes are toxic to horses too, so don't plant them in or near your field.

If you don't know what plants to look for, contact the National Animal Poison Control Center (see appendix). The NAPCC publishes a booklet called *Natural Poisons in Horses*, which you can purchase and use as a reference tool.

will flap around and alert your horse that the wire is there.

Never ever put your horse in a field with barbed wire fencing. It is extremely dangerous and can cause serious injury.

Gates

A gate should be as tall as the surrounding fence, made of strong material, and locked securely with a horseproof latch. A clever horse can figure out how to open a gate and will do it over and over! You can buy horseproof latches at a tack store or from an agricultural merchant.

Water

A field must have a constant supply of clean, fresh water from a tap. A horse drinks 5 to 20 gallons of water a day—or more if it's hot, if she gets a lot of exercise, or eats alfalfa hay regularly. Without enough water, your horse could get dehydrated and sick.

Water can be kept in a purpose-made trough, a plastic barrel, or an old bathtub—provided it has no sharp edges or rust. You may have to fill it every day with a hose, or you can get a plumber to set up an automatic waterer with a valve.

Check the trough every day in the winter to make sure the water hasn't frozen, and break the ice if necessary. You might also put a big rubber ball in the trough. If your horse doesn't take it out and play with it, the ball should float around and keep the water from freezing.

Shelter

Some type of shelter is necessary in a field. Ideally, there should be a walk-in barn or shed. If not, the field should have some trees to offer cover from rain and give shade in the summer.

Space

The field should have at least one acre of room per horse. If you put too many horses in a small field, the grass will soon be eaten and the grazing ruined. If you have two fields, rotate the horses between them so the grasses have time to grow again.

ROUTINE FIELD CHECKS

If your horse is going to spend any time in a field, here are some jobs that you must be prepared to do on a regular basis.

Every Day

Check twice a day to make sure your horse is comfortable and free from injuries—don't just wave at her from the other side of the fence. Go in and take a closer look. Clean out her hooves with a hoof pick. If she wears shoes, make sure they're still on. If a shoe is missing, try to find it. If it has nails sticking out, a horse could step on them and get a serious puncture wound.

Check the water supply and clean out the trough. Old leaves and rubbish can make the water taste bad, and a horse might not want to drink.

A field must have a fresh water supply.

Every Week

Go into the field and shovel piles of manure onto a muck heap. This isn't the most glamorous job in the world, but it keeps your horse's grazing in good shape. Horses are fussy eaters and tend to avoid grass that has manure on it.

Manure also attracts pesky flies and is a terrific home for worm eggs. You could pay a local farmer to rake the field with a tractor and spread the manure.

Check all the fences and make sure they're not broken. Pick up any rubbish that has blown into the field.

Picking up manure piles can cut down on flies.

A pen should be partially covered.

PENS

In some parts of the United States, especially the Southwest, many people house their horses in pens or corrals. A pen for a single horse should be at least 12 feet x 24 feet in size, and partially covered so the horse has shelter from the elements. It should have a soft, thick bedding of shavings or sand, with new bedding added a couple times a month. If your horse lies down, she won't be comfortable on a hard dirt floor, nor will she stay clean. A pen must be mucked out every day. It should also have a steady supply of water. If yours has an automatic waterer, check it every day to make sure it's working properly.

STABLES

A stable must be big enough for a horse to walk around and lie down. A 12-foot x 10-foot stable is suitable for a pony up to 14.2hh, but a horse needs an area 12 feet x 12 feet or more. The ceiling should be at least 10 feet from the ground so your horse won't bang her head if she rears.

The stable must have a large door, at least 4 feet wide, with plenty of space to pass through. For safety reasons, it should open outward. Most stable doors are divided so you can close the bottom and open the top, allowing your horse to look out and get some air. It's best to have two bolts on the door—one at the top and one at the bottom.

A stable should be well ventilated, preferably with a window to let in fresh air. Protect the window glass on the inside with strong wire mesh or bars. Keep the barn doors open. If the barn is constantly sealed tight, dust can cause breathing problems. A light is necessary, but it must be covered and out of your horse's reach. A stable should also have two sturdy metal rings bolted into the wall—one for a hay net and one to tie your horse to when you groom her.

Bedding

You must cover the stable floor with soft, comfortable bedding because standing on hard cement or a dirt floor can cause leg sores and lameness. Deep bedding prevents drafts and keeps a horse warm if she lies down. To test if you have enough bedding, stick a pitchfork in. You shouldn't be able to feel the ground. Try for at least a foot of bedding. Here are two common types of bedding you'll find at your local tack or feed store.

Wood Shavings or Sawdust: Many people use shavings or sawdust in their stable because both are comfortable for a horse to lie on and fairly easy to keep clean. These are low in dust and are excellent bedding for a horse with breathing problems or allergies. They come in big plastic or paper sacks and are more expensive than other types of bedding.

Straw: Straw is the least expensive bedding. It comes in open bales tied with twine. You'll need several bales to fill a stable. Store straw in a dry place; it gets moldy when wet and can make a horse ill. Straw can also be dusty and make a horse cough. Spend enough money for the best straw available. Keep an eye on your horse's weight if she has straw in her stable because many horses find it tasty and munch on it.

A stable should be comfortable and roomy.

Sawdust is fairly easy to keep clean.

Mucking Out

You must clean, or muck out, a stable every day. This is when you remove the manure and wet patches and leave behind unsoiled bedding. Most people find it easiest to do one big muck-out a day.

If you do not clean a stable regularly, it will become dirty, smelly, and unhygienic, and your horse and her blankets will be impossible to keep clean. Wet bedding can give your horse thrush, a nasty hoof infection.

You need certain tools to muck out a stall. You can buy them at a tack shop or hardware store. Keep them in a safe place where a horse (or human) can't step on them and get hurt. You need:

🐎 A broom

🐎 A pitchfork

🐎 A rake

🐎 A wheelbarrow or big muck bucket

Here's what to do every day to keep your horse's stable fresh and clean:

1. Turn out your horse into a field or ring. It will be much easier to clean her stable if she's out of your way. Then use the pitchfork to lift out wet patches and droppings. Once the pitchfork is loaded, shake it gently so clean bedding falls off and stays in the stable. Toss the dirty bedding into the wheelbarrow or muck bucket.

A stable will stay fresher if you pick out droppings as they appear. Take five minutes to lift out new piles before you say "good night" to your horse and you'll have a cleaner horse in the morning.

2. Empty the dirty bedding on a muck heap, as far away from the stable as possible because it smells bad and attracts flies. Try to keep the muck heap neat and tidy. Arrange to have it taken away at least once a month by a garbage service, or pay a farmer to haul it away. A farmer can spread it on his or her fields as fertilizer.

Lift out wet patches and droppings.

*A muck heap should be
far away from the stable.*

4. Leave the stable empty to air for a few hours.

5. Use the pitchfork to add plenty of new bedding to the stable floor. Don't skimp! Mix it with the old bedding. Rake the bedding flat in the middle of the stable, and bank it (make it higher) around the walls. Banking prevents your horse from lying too close to the wall and getting cast (stuck), which can require several people to pull the horse away from the wall so that she can stand up again.

6. Finally, clean your horse's feed manger and rinse out her water bucket and refill it with fresh water.

3. Sweep or rake the remaining bedding close to the walls. Leave the middle of the floor and any other wet patches clear so they'll dry while your horse is out for the day. Sprinkle lime powder on the wet spots. Lime powder absorbs urine and deodorizes the stable. You can buy it at a tack shop or at a farm-, agricultural-, or building-supply store.

*Clean out water buckets
every day.*

STABLE VICES

If a horse stays in her stable too much she can get bored and acquire bad habits known as stable vices. The most common stable vices are cribbing, weaving, pawing, and stable kicking.

Cribbing

Cribbing is the act of chewing wood in the stable or out in the field. Many horses like to chew wood, but cribbing refers to an involuntary, automatic reaction to boredom or nervousness. The horse grabs on to wood, metal—anything—with her teeth, arches her neck, and swallows air. Because the activity releases endorphins, which relax the horse, the behavior is almost impossible to stop.

*Cribbing can damage
a horse's teeth.*

Swallowing pieces of wood can give your horse a stomachache, and chewing wood can damage her teeth permanently. To stop her from cribbing in her stable, paint all chewable wood or other surfaces with a bad-tasting, horse-safe coating (available at a feed store) or cover the top half of the bottom door with a strip of metal to protect the wood from gnawing teeth.

Alternatively, you can make your horse wear a cribbing strap, a special collar made of leather and metal that makes it hard for her to grab the wood. Make sure you take it off for a couple of hours every day to prevent sores.

Weaving

Weaving is when your horse swings her neck and head from side to side and shifts her weight from one leg to another as she stands in the stable doorway. Weaving makes a nervous horse feel more secure. You must put a special U-shaped stall screen on her door so she can look out but not weave.

Pawing

Some horses paw the floor in their stable when they get excited or impatient. It usually happens around feed time. Pawing can damage your floor and wear down your horse's front shoes. Put a thick rubber mat in front of her door, where she probably paws the most.

Stable Kicking

Horses kick the wall of their stable when they're bored and want some human attention, when they're excited, and when they're not feeling friendly to the horse next door. To cut down on the noise and prevent injury, hang a thick rubber mat on the wall. Yelling when she does it might do the trick too!

Feeding a Horse

IF YOUR HORSE HAD HIS WAY, HE'D LIVE IN A huge field with plenty of tasty, nutritious grass to nibble. In this case, he knows best. Grass has almost all the vitamins and nutrients a horse needs to stay healthy. In the wild, horses can live quite happily on an unlimited supply of grass and water. But humans have domesticated horses and altered their lifestyle. Instead of living on grassy plains, they are kept in fields, pens, and stables, without enough or any grass. And instead of lazing about on their own, we make them gallop around barrels and jump fences. All of this athletic activity requires extra energy so their dietary needs have changed.

A horse must be fed and watered every day, and as his owner, you need to know exactly what he should eat and how much, even if you don't feed him yourself. If fed properly, he'll have a shiny, healthy coat and plenty of energy. If not, he'll look thin and run-down and won't perform to his potential. But if he gets too much to eat, he'll get flabby and sluggish, and the extra pounds may put stress on his legs and make him lame.

When you buy a horse, ask the owner to write down the type of feed the horse has been eating and when he is fed. Keeping his diet the same makes his move less stressful.

If you can't find out this information, ask your instructor—or a friend who has a horse of similar size and age—to suggest a suitable diet.

At some boarding facilities, you may not have much say about what your horse eats, especially if every horse gets the same food. This can be frustrating for the conscientious owner, but if you visit your horse daily, you can give him more food or a supplement if he needs one.

To learn more about feeds, talk to a feed merchant and read some feed sacks for information about the food inside and the sort of horses they suit. Look around the barn to see what feeds other people feed their horses. Find out what kind of hay people feed too. This may vary from area to area.

FEEDING RULES

Here are ten time-honored feeding rules that every responsible horse owner should follow:

1. Feed little and often. Horses have tiny stomachs so their often-delicate digestive system works best when they eat small amounts of food throughout the day. This is why it's better to feed a horse several small meals a day instead of one or even two. Three meals is best, especially if your horse is stabled all the time.

In the wild, horses graze continuously, which keeps their digestive system working smoothly. If your horse is fortunate, he spends some time each day out in a field and can eat grass. If he lives in a pen or stable, give him hay to snack on.

*Grass is the most natural food
for a horse.*

Never give your horse too much food. This can cause colic, a serious equine stomachache. Horses aren't like humans. They don't stop eating when they are full, and they can't throw up. *If a horse overeats, the food can cause intestinal blockages that can kill him.* This is why you must lock the feed-room door so your horse can't get in and stuff himself silly.

2. Always have fresh water available. Your horse must have an unlimited supply of water in his field or stable. If he doesn't get enough, he could become dehydrated or lose his appetite. Offer your horse water before you feed him. If you give it to him after he eats, he may gulp it down and wash the food through his digestive system too quickly. Excess water also causes some types of grains to swell in a horse's stomach, which can cause colic.

Don't let your horse drink too much after hard exercise. Let him cool down first, and then he can have only a few sips. Very cold water can shock the system of an overheated horse.

3. Feed at regular times. Horses are creatures of habit. They like knowing when they're going to be fed each day. It gives them a sense of security. Feeding late or inconsistently can worry a horse and make him sick. If you're going away, tell the person taking care of your horse what time to feed him.

4. Make diet changes gradually. Horses have sensitive stomachs, and sudden changes can cause colic. Mix the old food with the new for a few days, and then gradually increase the proportion of the new food. If you change his hay, for example, from alfalfa to grass, feed a combination of the two for a few days, then gradually finish off the old hay and continue feeding the new.

Introduce pasture grass slowly, especially in the spring when it is richest. If your horse has been inside all winter, eating too much spring grass could give him laminitis (founder), a nasty disease that poisons a horse's blood and causes lameness. Feed him hay before you turn him out, and let him graze for only about an hour or so at first. If he seems okay, gradually increase the time he spends in the field.

A horse can drink more than 13 gallons of water each day.

5. Feed a lot of roughage (food with fiber). Fiber comes from foods such as hay and grass. A horse's digestive system requires fiber to keep it working smoothly. If your horse is stabled all the time—or has bare pasture—feed him fiber each day in the form of hay or hay cubes.

6. Feed top quality, fresh food. Feed your horse the best quality food you can afford.

Remove grain from its sack and store it in a metal bin or plastic garbage can so it stays fresh and free of hungry mice. Keep the lid securely fastened so your horse can't get in either.

Store hay off the ground on wooden pallets, and keep it covered so it doesn't get wet and moldy. Damp or dusty food can make your horse sick. Keep buckets and mangers clean. Scrub them regularly to keep germs away.

A horse's digestive system needs fibrous foods such as hay.

Store feed in a rodent-proof container.

7. Feed succulents. Add something succulent (juicy) to your horse's feed every day. Apples and carrots are tasty and add variety and moisture to his diet.

8. Give your horse salt. Put a salt block in your horse's field or stable so he can lick it whenever he wants. Salt is an essential mineral; a horse loses it when he sweats during exercise or in hot weather. Some feeds have salt in them, but if your horse does a lot of work in warm weather, he may need more. There are two common types of block you will find at the tack store—pure white salt and a reddish-brown salt with minerals added.

9. Wait an hour after feeding before exercise. Your horse needs about an hour to digest his

Wait about an hour after a horse has eaten before riding him.

food properly before you ride him. The blood supply to a horse's muscles increases during exercise, causing the blood supply to his digestive system to decrease. This can upset your horse's digestion. If you have to interrupt your horse's breakfast, lunch, or dinner to ride, keep the exercise short and nonstrenuous.

10. Feed according to need. Every horse is different, so it's best to learn your horse's individual feeding needs. Obviously, a small pony is going to eat less than a large horse, and a horse who gets a lot of work needs more food than one who doesn't get ridden at all. Here are some feeding guidelines:

There are special feeds for different ages.

A horse in a pen or stable has different dietary needs from a horse in a field.

Too much feed can make a nervous horse behave badly.

Feed according to size. Buy a special measuring tape at the tack shop and use it to estimate your horse's weight.

Feed according to type. A fuzzy mixed-breed has different dietary needs from a thin-skinned, purebred Arabian.

Horses need more food in the winter because it takes a lot of energy to keep warm.

The harder your horse works, the more feed he needs.

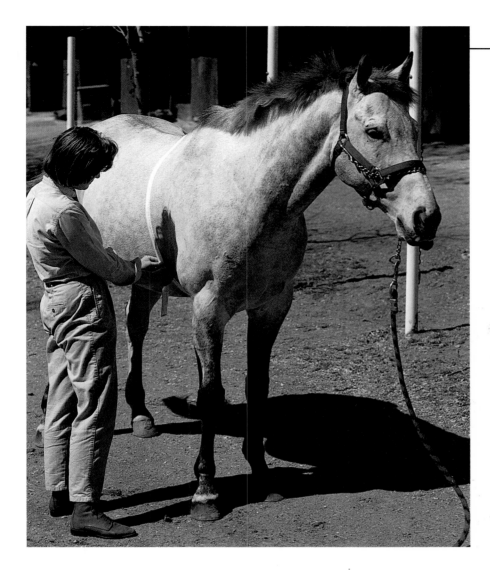

Use a special measuring tape to figure out your horse's approximate weight.

FOOD TO FEED A HORSE

There are two groups of horse feeds that you need to know about: concentrates and roughage. Your horse needs both in his diet to keep him healthy.

Roughage

Roughage is grass, hay, and hay cubes or pellets. A horse needs a lot of roughage to keep his digestive system working properly. Grass is the most natural type of food for horses. Different types of grass grow in different climates and the quality of grass can vary from field to field.

Most horses get the bulk of their roughage from hay, which is grass that has been cut and dried, usually in the summer when it's most nutritious. Hay is usually stored in bales. If a horse doesn't get much work, he may thrive on a diet of hay only—provided that the hay is nutritious. Buy hay at a feed store or from a local farmer. The type and quality varies from area to area. Ask your stable mates where they purchase high-quality hay. The most commonly found types of hay are:

Grass Hay: Grass hay is a low-energy, filling, and fairly inexpensive hay and can be made from a variety of grasses.

Alfalfa Hay: Energy-giving, it is very nutritious, but can be too rich for some horses and is expensive.

Oat Hay: Oat hay is low-energy, filling, and usually inexpensive.

Timothy: Timothy is low-energy, moderately nutritious grass hay.

Bermuda Hay: This grass hay is similar to Timothy in nutritional value.

Only buy hay that is greenish-yellow and smells sweet. Give it a good sniff before you feed it to your horse. Hay that is dusty, yellow, or moldy can make a horse ill. Some folks like to put their hay in a net and soak it in clean water for a few hours. Soaking hay removes some of the dust that can irritate a horse's lungs, and the hay can be eaten wet.

Horses prefer to eat hay off the ground, but this can be wasteful—plus you don't want your horse to ingest a lot of dirt. Put the hay in some sort of manger.

Hay can be ground up, dried, and compressed into cubes or pellets. If you can't get good hay in your area, cubes are an excellent substitute because they're as nutritious as loose hay. Fussy horses may find them awkward to eat, but in some facilities, hay cubes are the only feed given to the horses.

Give hay a sniff to make sure it is fresh, not moldy.

Hay cubes are a source of roughage.

Concentrates

Concentrates are foods that are high in nutritional value and fed in small amounts. They can be grain, mixed feeds, or pellets. Concentrates are sometimes called "hard feed."

Use concentrates when your horse's nutritional needs are not being met by eating hay or grass. For example, if you're working your horse hard, he may not be getting enough energy from hay alone. If you want him to gain weight, you may have to feed him concentrates. A pregnant mare or a mare with a foal usually needs to eat concentrates to stay healthy.

If your horse is retired or doesn't get much work, he probably doesn't need concentrates. If he's too energetic or nervous, decrease or eliminate his concentrates altogether. You'll come across some different kinds of concentrates.

Grains: Oats, corn, barley, and bran are the most common concentrates. Oats are high in energy; corn is full of protein; barley is good for adding weight; and bran acts as a laxative. Experienced horse people sometimes mix grains to make their own hard feeds, but you have to be knowledgeable about equine nutrition and different grains' qualities before you attempt this.

Complete Feeds and Pellets: Complete feeds are usually a mixture of grains such as barley, oats, and corn. They also contain all of the vitamins and minerals a horse needs. They are developed by equine nutritionists and are easy to use because manufacturers specify on the product the amount to feed your horse. The amounts are usually in pounds, so get a scale from a feed supply store or horse supply catalog and a big can or scoop to use to measure your feed accurately. If you're a new horse owner, or simply want an uncomplicated life, feed your horse a complete feed or pellets. Combined with hay or grass, complete feeds or pellets should give your horse a well-rounded diet.

There are plenty complete feeds and pellets to choose from at the feed store, and the feed companies make different feeds to suit different types of horses. There are special feeds for pregnant mares, mares in foal, young horses, performance horses, and senior citizens. The most popular complete feeds seem to be "sweet feeds," mixtures that contain different types of grain moistened with molasses to make them extra tasty.

Pellets are a mixture of crushed grains, vitamins, and minerals. They can be bland and dry, though, and some horses find them boring to eat. Throw a few carrots and apples in with them to spice up your horse's mealtimes.

Sweet feed contains vitamins and nutrients needed by a horse.

VITAMINS AND SUPPLEMENTS

If your horse eats a complete multigrain feed, he may be getting all the vitamins and minerals he needs. The information on the sack should state if the feed satisfies a horse's daily nutritional requirements. But if your horse eats only hay or hay cubes, he may need a daily vitamin or mineral supplement, which you can find at a tack shop. They come in powder or pellet form, and you add them to your horse's meals each day. Some supplements include biotin, a vitamin that strengthens hooves. Others contain cod liver oil to make your horse's coat shiny. A less-expensive way to bring out the shine in your horse's coat is to add a dollop of corn oil (about a quarter cup each day) to each of your horse's feeds. Corn oil contains fat so it can also help a thin horse gain weight.

Electrolytes are supplements generally given to competition horses. They combine minerals—including chloride, sodium, and potassium—that your horse needs to stay healthy. If your horse has access to a salt block and a nutritious diet, it's unlikely he will need electrolytes—especially if he doesn't work very hard. If he does a lot of work—for instance, he's a three-day eventer or an endurance horse—he may need these minerals replenished after strenuous exercise. Horses who live in hot climates and sweat a lot may also need them.

Electrolytes usually come in powder form and are mixed into a horse's water. Do not use electrolytes unless your vet says that your horse needs them.

Cut carrots into finger-size segments and apples into quarters.

*Hold your hand flat when
feeding treats.*

TREATS

Horses love carrots and apples, which are good for them. You can buy special horse treats that look like cookies, but don't give your horse candy or sugar cubes. They're bad for his teeth. Cut apples into quarters and carrots into finger-size segments to make them easy for your horse to chew. Smaller pieces can get stuck in his throat and choke him.

Giving treats by hand is a bad idea because your horse will come to expect them and may bite or bother you for them. Be sensible and feed treats in a bucket. If you must feed a treat by hand, when you are catching your horse, for example, hold your hand flat and put the treat on it. Never hold the treat with your fingers because your horse may nibble them instead of the tidbit.

A Horse's Health

Your horse should have her own equine veterinarian, someone you trust who knows your horse inside and out. Choose a local vet who can get to your horse quickly in an emergency.

If you keep your horse at a boarding facility, put a card on her stall door with the names and numbers of both you and your vet. A passer-by who notices your horse is ill can call you both. But don't count on others to make sure your horse is healthy, especially at a big, busy barn. It's your responsibility. Check your horse every day to make sure she is okay. This means looking at her from head to hoof.

Here are signs that tell you your horse is feeling great:

She's alert and interested in everything going on around her.

Her ears move around and listen for interesting sounds.

She eats all of her food.

She has a shiny coat.

Her legs and hooves are cool to the touch.

She puts weight on all four feet.

Her droppings are firm and ball-shaped.

Here are signs that tell you to call the vet:

Your horse looks depressed and hangs her head low.

She's listless and doesn't move around.

She doesn't eat or finish her food.

She doesn't drink water.

She limps and keeps her weight off a particular leg.

She coughs or has a runny nose or eyes.

A healthy horse looks great and has plenty of energy.

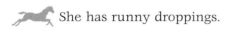 She has runny droppings.

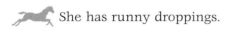 Her coat is dull and has bare patches.

 She nips at her stomach or rolls violently (signs of colic).

TAKING YOUR HORSE'S TEMPERATURE

If you suspect your horse is sick, take her temperature. It's not difficult. Keep a veterinary thermometer in your tack box. It should have a long safety string with a clip on the end. If it doesn't, tie on a long ribbon or piece of string with a clothespin on the end of it. Clip the ribbon or string to your horse's tail so the thermometer can't disappear inside her or fall on the ground.

A horse's temperature should be between 100 and 101° F.

Touch her neck to see if you can feel a lumpy obstruction. If you can, call the vet immediately, and encourage the horse to drink some water, which may push the food down her throat.

Prevent choking by giving your horse an unlimited supply of water, cutting carrots and apples into easy-to-chew sizes, and placing bricks or big rocks in your horse's manger to prevent her from gulping food.

Colic

Colic is an equine stomachache caused by many things, including:

🐎 A change in the weather

🐎 A change of feed

🐎 Damage to her stomach or intestines caused by worms

🐎 Overeating

🐎 Swallowing dirt or sand along with feed

🐎 Stress

Shake the thermometer so it reads below 97 degrees Fahrenheit. To insert it easily, dip the thermometer in petroleum jelly. Lift your horse's tail and gently slide the thermometer into her rectum, leaving about half of it outside. Keep it in place for two minutes, then take it out, wipe it clean, and read it. The temperature of a healthy horse should be between 100° F and 101° F. If it is any higher or lower and the horse has symptoms of distress, call the vet.

HEALTH PROBLEMS
Choking

Choking is caused by something getting stuck in your horse's esophagus. It can happen when you feed her large, lumpy foods such as hay cubes, which she may not chew properly. If a horse is choking, she stops eating and may panic. She drools, and food may come out her nose.

A horse with colic may pace around her stall. She may nip or kick at her stomach, or lie down and roll. Sometimes her only symptoms are lethargy and depression. When you call the vet, describe the behavior and she will tell you what to do until she arrives.

You may have to walk the horse. Gentle exercise can help the feed to move through her digestive system. It's a good sign if she passes wind or makes droppings because she will soon feel better. If your horse seems depressed, leave her alone. Don't force her to walk, but if she's cold, blanket her.

If your horse is rolling violently, then the colic is serious. Get her up on her feet right away. Rolling can twist her intestines and kill her. When the vet arrives, he or she may give your horse a tranquilizer if she's upset or moving around too much. Then the vet may drench the horse's intestines with mineral oil. This involves running a hose down her nose and pumping mineral oil into her stomach. The oil helps to ease dangerous food blockages through a horse's digestive system, and she should recover in a couple of hours.

Heaves
(sometimes called
emphysema or dust allergy)

Heaves is a lung condition that makes it hard for a horse to breathe properly. Sometimes when a horse eats moldy, dusty hay or continually lives in dusty surroundings, her lungs become weak and she must use her stomach muscles to push the air out of her lungs. An affected horse heaves when she breathes, and coughs a lot. Sadly, a horse with heaves cannot be cured and lacks the stamina to become a competition star. But, if you soak her hay in water, wet her feed, and keep her home dust-free, she may be able to do light work.

Lameness

Signs of lameness are limping and trying to take weight off one leg. The horse may also bob her head up and down when she moves or be extra bumpy when you ride her. Before you call the vet, check her legs for the following:

A cut that needs to be cleaned and medicated

A rock or other debris, such as a nail, stuck in the hoof. Use a hoof pick to get rid of debris, then soak the hoof in $^3/_4$ cup of Epsom salts mixed in a bucket of warm water for 15 minutes. This soothes minor soreness.

Stone bruises. These are common and happen when your horse steps on a rock or another hard object and bruises her sole or heel. Soak the area in $^3/_4$ cup of Epsom salts mixed in a bucket of warm water for 15 minutes several times over a couple of days, and put some "bute" (equine aspirin) in her feed. If the soreness doesn't go away after a few days, call the vet.

Loose nails from her shoes or nails sticking into the sensitive hoof wall. An outgrown shoe could be pinching her feet. In this case, call the farrier to remove the shoe, or pull it off yourself if you know how.

Lumps that could be splints. Splints are bony growths on the lower leg, usually caused by working a young horse too hard. When splints are new, they can be painful, so rest your horse for a while. If the lameness goes away, it's unlikely the splint will cause more damage—but it will look unsightly. If the lameness continues, the splint may need veterinary attention.

🐎 A pulled muscle. The vet will have to examine the horse to find out what is causing the lameness.

🐎 Always rest a lame horse, and if the condition persists, put her in a stable that restricts her movement and call the vet.

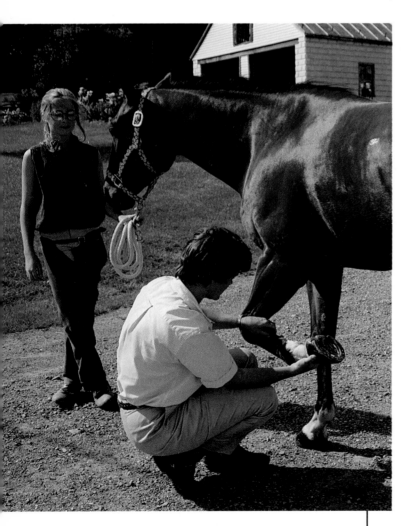

If a horse is lame, the vet will check the leg for suspicious lumps.

Laminitis (founder)

Laminitis is a serious metabolic condition that can make a horse lame. It is usually caused by overeating, such as when a horse eats too much rich grass or breaks into the feed room and stuffs herself silly. Laminitis releases toxins into the bloodstream that travel down to the hooves and damage the circulation of the feet. It affects either the front feet or all four. The laminae, which is the sensitive tissue that attaches the hoof wall to the horse's coffin bone, becomes inflamed, and the horse suffers great pain. Her hooves feel hot, rings may appear around her hoof wall, and her toes may curl up. She may lean backward to take her weight off her hooves.

If you think your horse has laminitis, remove her feed and call the vet. She may tell you to hose the hooves until she arrives. Then she may put a horse with laminitis in a special "diet" field with little grass, or she may cut down her feed and prescribe medicine. Sadly, once a horse suffers a laminitis attack, you have to be careful about her diet because it can recur.

Mud Fever (cracked heels)

If your horse lives in a muddy field or her stable is often wet, her heels or pasterns can get chapped and sore and start splitting. If this happens, keep her footing as dry as possible, and her pastern and heels clean. Trim stray hairs away from the infected area and apply an antibacterial ointment.

To prevent mud fever, keep your horse's heels dry. Don't hose off her legs every day, especially in the winter. If her legs get muddy, wait for them to dry, then brush them off. It may help to apply petroleum jelly to her heels in wet weather.

Navicular Disease

If your horse is constantly lame, she may have navicular disease—a painful condition that affects the navicular bone inside the hoof and the attached tendon. Both become inflamed, causing soreness in the hoof. A horse with navicular takes short, stiff steps. The condition can be caused by:

Bad shoeing

Lack of regular hoof care

Poor hoof and leg conformation

Too much work on hard footing

If your horse is diagnosed with navicular disease, your farrier may put special shoes on her to make her more comfortable, and she may require regular medicine. Don't give up on a horse with navicular disease because she may be able to continue to do light work.

Ringworm

Ringworm is a nasty fungus that causes your horse's hair to fall out in the shape of a circle. It is highly contagious to you and other animals, so isolate her and wash your hands and tools in a disinfectant solution after touching her. Don't use her brushes and blankets on any other horses. Your vet should give you an antibacterial cream and a medicated wash to use on the infected area.

Thrush

Thrush is a bacterial disease that affects the frog area—the V-shaped cleft in the hoof. Horses who stand in wet or dirty footing are likely to get thrush. It's easy to spot because the infected hoof has a bad odor, and the frog is crumbly and covered in a gooey, black substance.

If your horse gets thrush, keep her hooves completely dry. Your vet or farrier may tell you to soak the hoof in an antibacterial solution or apply medicine to the infected area.

The easiest way to avoid thrush is to pick out your horse's hooves every day and keep her stable or pen clean and dry.

REGULAR VETERINARY CHECKUPS

The best way to maintain a healthy horse is to have regular vet checkups. Once or twice a year is usually enough. The vet listens to your horse's heart and takes her temperature. She checks her legs to make sure they are free of injuries.

One of the most important things the vet should do on a regular basis is float, or rasp, your horse's teeth. She uses a big metal file to level out any sharp edges on your horse's teeth so she can eat properly. Once a year is usually enough, but young and old horses may need more frequent floatings.

Inoculations and Tests

When your vet comes for a checkup, she also vaccinates your horse. Vaccinations vary from area to area, depending on which viruses exist in your state. If you plan to show your horse, she'll need certain shots, and show organizers often ask you to bring your veterinary records so they can check that she has had her shots. Here are some shots or tests the vet may give your horse:

Tetanus (lockjaw): Tetanus is an infection of the nervous system that can happen if a horse steps on a rusty nail or gets a deep cut. The horse's muscles stiffen so badly that she can barely move. Most tetanus cases are fatal. A shot is given once a year.

Influenza (flu): The flu is a contagious, air-borne virus. When one horse has the flu, it is likely that others at the facility will get it too. A horse with flu has a runny nose and may cough. Two or three shots a year is normal.

A horse needs his teeth rasped at least once a year.

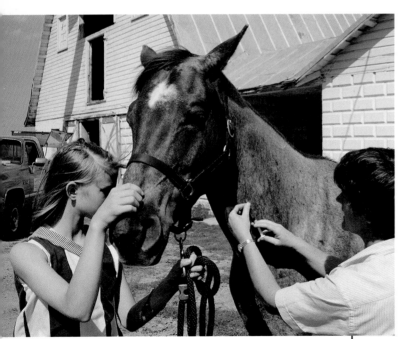

Equine vaccinations vary from area to area.

Encephalomyelitis (sleeping sickness): This deadly virus is carried by mosquitoes. A horse contracts a serious fever and then becomes paralyzed. A yearly vaccination is usually recommended.

Rabies: If there have been cases of animals with rabies in your area, your vet may vaccinate your horse against the disease. Luckily, horses rarely get rabies.

Equine Infectious Anemia (swamp fever): This is another deadly virus that lives in a horse's blood and is passed from horse to horse by biting insects, such as mosquitoes. Unfortunately, there is no vaccination at this time for this disease, but there is a test called a Coggins test that shows if your horse has been exposed to the virus. Many show organizers will ask to see your Coggins test results. If your horse is a carrier of the virus, she has to be put down.

WORMING

Horses are constantly exposed to internal parasites (worms), so they must be dewormed on a regular basis. Worms can damage a horse's blood vessels, intestines, lungs, and heart. A horse with worm infestation is thin and sickly because most of the parasites live in the digestive tract and make it difficult for the horse to process food effectively. Wormy horses often suffer colic attacks.

Generally, parasites lay eggs in a horse's stomach. The eggs then travel through the digestive system and come out in the manure. They hatch into tiny larvae that crawl onto blades of grass. A horse eats the grass, and the cycle starts again.

Here are some worms that can make your horse ill:

Large strongyles (bloodworms) and small strongyles damage a horse's blood vessels, digestive system, and other internal organs. They sometimes cause colic, which can kill a horse.

Ascarids live in a horse's small intestine and are often found in foals and young horses.

Pinworms irritate a horse's rectum; an afflicted horse may rub her tail and rear end a lot.

Bot flies lay eggs on a horse's skin, usually around her legs, shoulders, and chin. They look like little yellow dots. When the eggs hatch, the larvae find their way to the horse's mouth and are swallowed. Some mature into bots, which stick to the stomach wall and cause ulcers. Others are expelled with manure and hatch into bot flies. If you see bot eggs on your horse, scrape them off carefully with a razor blade.

Deworm your horse on a regular schedule, usually every eight to twelve weeks. You can buy dewormer at a tack shop, from a catalog, or from your vet. There are different dewormers for different parasites, so ask your vet which one to use. Veterinarians usually recommend that you rotate dewormers because parasites can develop an immunity to certain wormers if they are used repeatedly.

Dewormers come in a powder, which is added to feed, or a paste. The pastes come in an oral syringe (no needle). The numbers on the side of the syringe tell you how much to give your horse, depending on her weight. (If you don't know how much your horse weighs, buy a special measuring tape to determine her approximate weight.) Set the plunger at your horse's weight. Hold her nose up high and stick the syringe into the corner of her mouth.

A paste dewormer is easy to use.

Then press the plunger so that the paste squirts onto the back of her tongue. Hold her head up for a minute after you remove the syringe so you can be sure she swallows the paste. Here are some other ways to prevent worms:

Remove manure piles from your horse's field on a regular basis.

Keep food away from manure.

Don't crowd too many horses into a tiny field or pen.

Rest a field (take the horses out) for a couple of months to break the worm's life cycle.

FIRST AID

Always be prepared for an emergency. Keep a first aid kit handy and post your vet's phone number where it can be easily seen. Here is what should be in your first aid kit:

Absorbent sheets of cotton and cotton balls

Adhesive tape

Clean sponges (a couple)

Disinfectant or antiseptic solution for cleaning cuts

Epsom salts

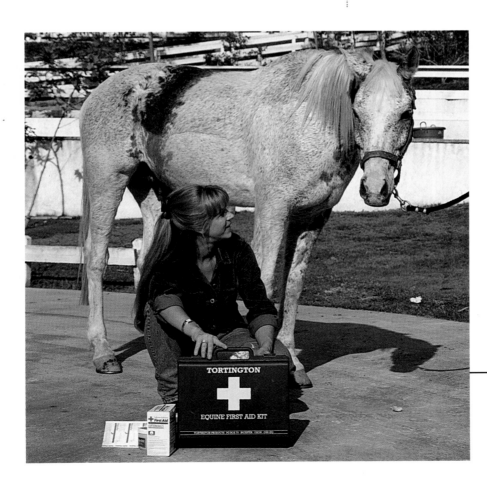

*Always keep
a first aid kit handy.*

Gauze roll and gauze squares

Saline solution

Scissors

Several rolls of stretch bandage

Veterinary thermometer

Wound powder, spray, or solution

Replace items as you use them.

Cuts and Scrapes

If a wound is small, you should be able to treat it yourself:

1. Dip a pad of gauze in clean water and gently wipe the wound clean, replacing the gauze when it gets dirty.

2. Apply first aid powder, spray, or solution on and around the cleansed wound to prevent infection and keep flies away. Don't put a bandage or dressing on a minor wound, which heals better if left uncovered.

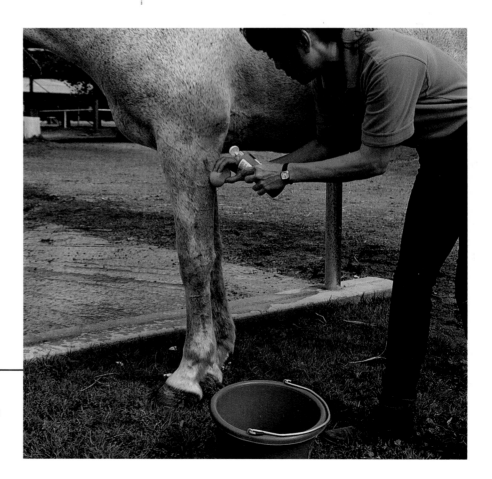

Clean small wounds thoroughly, then apply first aid powder or spray.

Serious Wounds

If a cut is deep and blood is spurting out of it, stay calm! Don't worry about cleaning it immediately. First, grab a large pad of gauze, fold it a few times, and press it firmly on the wound. Apply pressure while someone calls the vet. Sometimes pressure slows down the bleeding, and the wound can clot naturally. If the wound is on a leg, wrap a stretch bandage around the cotton and the wound, and secure it tightly with adhesive tape.

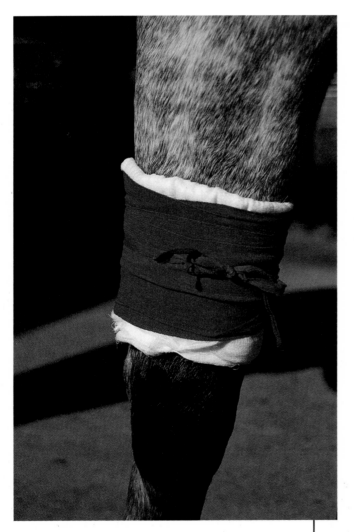

Use a bandage to apply pressure to a bleeding wound.

MODERN HEALTH THERAPIES

In recent years, there have been many advances in the field of equine health. Keep up with them by regularly reading horse magazines and chatting with your vet. Treatments such as chiropractic care, massage therapy, magnetic therapy, and acupuncture may benefit your horse in the future, so it is sensible to learn about these treatments now (before you need them). The following therapies should be used only on the advice of your vet:

Acupuncture and Acupressure

If a horse is in pain or ill, a veterinarian may recommend acupuncture. Fine needles are inserted into specific points on a horse's body to regulate her bodily functions. In simple terms, sticking needles into certain areas of a horse's body may make her feel better. Acupuncture has been used to treat lameness, arthritis, respiratory problems, and digestive disorders. It has also been used to control aggressive or nervous behavior in performance horses. It seems to calm them down.

Vets often combine acupuncture with more traditional therapies, such as antibiotics and anti-inflammatories (medicines that reduce swelling). Acupuncture should be done only by a qualified vet.

Acupresssure is when the vet or therapist uses his or her fingers—instead of needles—to massage the special points on a horse's body. It is usually used with acupuncture.

Chiropractic

Horses, like humans, suffer from back problems that can affect their performance and posture. Equine chiropractors believe that many problems stem from misalignments of the spine.

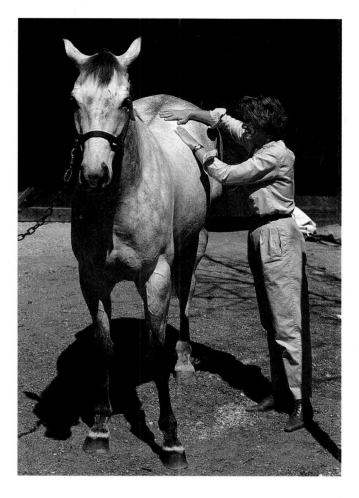

Acupressure can soothe aching muscles.

goal is to realign the spine so the nerves inside and around it can work properly.

More and more vets are becoming chiropractors, but if your vet doesn't practice it, ask him or her to recommend a qualified chiropractor. Only use someone with medical training.

Magnetic Therapy

Magnetic therapy is another method of treating injuries, mainly leg injuries, without drugs. A padded boot or wrap with bipolar magnets sewn inside it is placed over the injury. The magnetic field increases the blood flow around the injury, warms the skin, and delivers oxygen to the injured site, which speeds healing. The magnetic stimulation increases the flow of tissue materials and encourages new growth. It also removes waste products from an injury, which can help to relieve stiffness. Magnetic boots can be bought at a tack shop.

When the spine is not in its correct position, it may pinch nerves and make a horse uncomfortable. She may suffer muscle tightness, a loss of mobility, and decreased flexibility.

One benefit of chiropractic care is that it doesn't require drugs. Equine chiropractors restore normal movement and nerve function—when they can—by realigning a horse's spinal column with their hands, making short, controlled, thrusting movements to move the vertebrae. This is called an adjustment. A chiropractor may start at a horse's neck and then work down the spine to the tail. The chiropractor's

Massage Therapy

If a horse is stiff or sore, or has knots or cramps, sometimes a massage can loosen her up and make her feel better. A therapist firmly strokes the large muscles of the horse's neck, back, hips, and thighs. Massage relaxes the muscles so that normal circulation can return to them. Don't rely on massage therapy to cure your horse's ailments. It soothes a muscle problem for a while, but the pain usually returns. If your horse is continually sore, your vet must examine her to find out exactly what is wrong. Her soreness could be caused by a poorly fitting saddle or bad riding—both of which can be fixed without massage.

Massages should be given only by an equine massage therapist. They are not regulated, so be careful when choosing one. Ask horsey friends to recommend a good therapist.

GROOMING A HORSE

GROOMING IS THE WAY TO KEEP YOUR horse clean. You should groom him for a few minutes every day. The benefits of regular grooming are:

It cleans your horse's coat by removing dirt, sweat, dead skin cells, and excess hair. If mud and dirt remain on your horse's skin for long, they can cause rashes. A dirty coat is also a great home for fleas, ticks, and lice.

It improves your horse's circulation. All that brushing and rubbing is invigorating!

It brings the skin's natural oils to the surface, which makes a horse's coat look shiny.

It gives you a chance to examine your horse for cuts or bumps.

Always groom your horse *before* putting on his saddle and bridle. If your horse is dirty, the saddle and bridle will rub him and cause sores. Groom your horse after you ride, as well, to get rid of sweat and new dirt.

GROOMING KIT

Every horse owner needs a grooming kit—a box or bucket of brushes, sponges, and other tools necessary to keep your horse spic and span. You can buy these tools at a tack shop or order them from a catalog. Your grooming kit should contain these items:

Hoof Pick: A metal or plastic tool with a hook on one end to pick dirt and rocks out of a horse's hooves.

Curry Comb: A flexible rubber or plastic brush used to loosen dirt or mud on a horse's body. Metal curry combs are too sharp for a horse's skin, and should be used only to clean other brushes.

Dandy Brush: A brush with long, stiff bristles to remove dirt or dried mud that the curry comb has brought to the coat's surface

Body Brush: A soft brush with short bristles to remove surface dirt after you've used a curry comb and a dandy brush. A body brush is great for bringing out the shine in a horse's coat. Because it's soft, the body brush can be used on a horse's head and other sensitive places such as his stomach.

Grooming improves your horse's circulation.

Mane Comb: A small metal or plastic comb used to untangle a horse's mane and tail. There are also smaller combs for pulling a horse's mane. An inexpensive human hairbrush works great on the mane and tail too.

Stable Cloth: A soft cloth to remove stains or polish your horse's coat. Make a few by cutting an old towel into small squares.

Sponges: Your grooming kit should have several big, soft sponges. Use one for cleaning your horse's eyes and nose, and another for under his tail (the dock area). Using only one sponge for both areas spreads bacteria and infections. Use different colored sponges so you can tell them apart. Also buy a big general-purpose sponge for bath time.

Sweat Scraper: A plastic or metal tool to remove excess water from your horse after a bath so he dries more quickly

Water Brush: A brush with long, firm bristles to dampen the mane or tail. It is also used to clean mud from hooves.

Your grooming kit needs a good cleaning itself at least once a month. Use shampoo or detergent to wash your brushes and let them dry.

Use a rubber curry comb in circles.

GET GROOMING!

Tie your horse somewhere safe, away from other horses, using a safety knot (*see page 19*).

1. Start your grooming session by picking out your horse's hooves with the hoof pick.

2. Next, rub the curry comb in a circular motion on your horse's neck. Dirt and mud will rise to the coat's surface. Work your way back to the horse's hindquarters, but don't use a curry comb on sensitive areas such as the head or lower legs.

3. Use the dandy brush in short, firm strokes to sweep away the dirt you have turned up with the curry comb. Brush in the direction the hair grows. Start at the top of your horse's neck and work back to his hindquarters so you don't brush dirt onto parts you've already cleaned.

4. Next, use the soft body brush. It removes fine dirt and adds shine. Also use the body brush on your horse's head and lower legs. To clean the dandy brush and the body brush, scrape them on a metal curry comb and the dirt should fly off.

5. Dampen the eye/nose sponge with clean water, and gently wipe your horse's eyes and nose. Wet the other sponge and clean the dock area.

6. Finally, use your fingers to untangle the mane and tail. Then brush them with the hairbrush or a dandy brush. If you use a metal mane comb, be gentle because it can break the hair and cause equine frizzies. When you work on your horse's tail, stand to one side, not right behind the horse. If he spooks, you don't want to get stepped on or kicked.

7. If your horse has stains, dampen a stable cloth and remove them. Use a dry cloth to buff him, making his coat sleek and shiny. You can buy equine stain remover at tack shops; it's particularly handy if you have a gray horse (gray horse coats stain more easily).

A body brush can be used on sensitive places such as the face.

Keep your horse's eyes clean with a sponge.

Pulling the Mane

If you want your horse's mane to look neat and tidy, you may want to pull or thin it. For some breeds, such as Arabians, however, it's traditional to leave the mane (and tail) long and flowing. If you plan to show your horse in breed classes, find out what the requirements are before you start pulling.

Use your fingers or a small metal comb for pulling. Never use scissors on the mane because it will grow back unevenly and look ragged. Only pull a horse's mane after he has exercised—when he's warm and the pores of his skin are open. The hair pulls out more easily. Pull only for a few minutes at a time. Some horses really dislike having their manes pulled because it stings. Here's how you do it:

1. Start at the top of the neck. Comb or tease out a very small section of hair.

2. Wrap it around the comb and give a quick tug. The hair should come out.

3. Move down the neck, and repeat steps 1 and 2.

If your horse has a really long mane, try using a special trimming tool. It looks like a comb but has a razor inside and it costs only a couple of dollars. After combing the mane, break the ends of the hair off bit by bit with the razor part of the tool. Start at the top and work your way down the neck. Take only a little at first until you're sure you like the effect.

Trimming the Tail

If your horse's tail is extra thick, you may want to pull it as you would the mane. Remember to stand to the side of the horse so he can't kick you if this upsets him.

Some people like to pull the hairs at the top of the tail, to give it a smoother, neater effect. Others trim this area with clippers. Be warned, however, that once trimmed, the hair grows up and out and can look messy. You may find yourself in a grooming regimen you'll wish you never started. If you don't want to pull or trim the tail, you can tidy the hair at the top by wetting it down or putting hair gel on it.

You may want to trim the bottom of the tail, too. This is called "banging." The best way to do it is to brush the tail, then decide where you want to snip. Right under the scaly chestnuts on the inside of a horse's legs is the best spot. Hold up the tail and snip straight across. Put the tail down and even up the bottom with the scissors.

Trimming the Legs

If your horse has hairy legs, you might want to trim them. Simply brush the hair, called "feathers," then snip it off. It's best to cut up or down, rather than side to side, to give the hair a neater look. If your horse spends most of his time outdoors, leave the fetlock hair because rain runs off it without wetting your horse's heels.

Cutting a Bridle Path

Tidy up your horse's appearance by cutting a bridle path at the top of his mane. This allows the bridle to rest flat on his head. First, brush his mane. Then cut a path right behind his ears for the bridle to lie on. Clip the hair right down to his scalp. The path is usually about 1½ inches wide; however, different breeds have different requirements. Check with your breed society for showing rules.

Trimming the Head

If you want your horse to look super neat, trim the long hairs around his muzzle. These hairs act as feelers for a horse, but he can survive without them. You can also trim the hair around his ears. Squeeze both sides of the ear together and trim off the hair that is still sticking out. Leave the hair inside his ears alone. It keeps bugs and dirt out of the ear canal. Do not trim the long hairs around his eyes or his eyelashes.

A clipped horse dries off quickly after hard work.

Clipping

In cold weather, most horses grow long coats to keep warm; however, if a horse does a lot of work, a thick coat can be a problem. When he sweats, it can take a long time for his coat to dry, and he might get a chill. For this reason, many owners remove some or all of their horse's coat with electric clippers. A clipped horse dries quickly, is easier to keep clean, and generally looks neater than an unclipped one. But if you clip your horse, he needs to wear a blanket in his stable and a turn-out sheet or blanket in his field. If you don't ride your horse much in the winter or he lives outdoors all the time, don't clip him. He needs his coat to keep him cozy.

Tips for Clipping

Read the clipper manual before you begin, and always start with a clean, dry horse.

Get your horse used to the sound of clippers. Spend time just running the clippers near him before you start your work.

Allow plenty of time. Clipping takes awhile and your hastiness may upset your horse.

Clip against the direction of the hair.

Oil the clippers regularly to keep them working well and to prevent overheating.

Feel the clipper head frequently. If it's hot, turn the clippers off for a few minutes to cool them down.

BATH TIME

You shouldn't bathe your horse often because water and shampoo depletes a horse's coat of natural oils. Bathe your horse only if you have to, and make sure it's a fairly warm day when you do. You can buy special horse shampoo at a tack shop or use a mild shampoo for humans.

Start by hosing your horse's feet and legs to get him used to the water spray and temperature. Then hose down the front of his chest and around to his shoulders. Only after you have

Frequent shampooing can strip a horse's coat of needed oils.

thoroughly wetted his front section should you hose his back or stomach. Never spray water directly on a horse's face.

Next, lather him up with shampoo and a wet sponge. Be careful not to get soap in his eyes. Shampoo his mane and tail too. When you've finished scrubbing, thoroughly rinse the shampoo out of his coat. Then, use the sweat scraper to remove the excess water from his neck, back, stomach, and hindquarters. If it's a cool day, use a towel to dry off his face and legs.

If you're going to a show, bathe your horse a day or two beforehand. Washing removes the coat oil, and it will be at least twenty-four hours before his coat looks shiny again.

Cleaning the Sheath and Udders

If you have a gelding, it's essential that you clean his sheath area every other month. Smegma, a build-up of dead cells, urine, and dirt, collects in the sheath and can cause infections. To clean the sheath, you'll need a bucket of warm water, a mild soap or commercial sheath cleaner, a small sponge, and rubber gloves. Wet the sponge and squeeze some soap on it. Use the sponge to slowly clean in and around the sheath area. You should spot small chunks of black or gray smegma coming loose and falling out of the sheath. When you're done, rinse the sheath area with warm, clean water. Try your best to get all of the soap out, because it can cause an irritation if left behind.

Ask the vet to clean the sheath during your horse's annual checkup. He'll tranquilize your horse to encourage him to relax and drop his penis. Then he can thoroughly clean the sheath and penis.

If you have a mare, clean her udders with warm water and a sponge when you bathe her normally. Use soap infrequently in this area because it may cause irritation if overused.

FAREWELL TO FLIES

In warm weather your horse will be bugged by flies. You can buy fly repellent as a spray or liquid; wipe on the liquid with a rag. It also comes in a roll-on bottle to use around your horse's eyes and nose. Here are some handy tips to keep your horse free of flies:

Wipe your horse's eyes with a damp sponge and use fly repellent on him every day.

Put fly repellent around cuts on your horse's skin. Cuts attract flies.

Add a teaspoon of powdered garlic to his feed. Garlic is absorbed into his body and comes out in sweat. Flies don't like garlic.

Use a fly mask and/or fly socks.

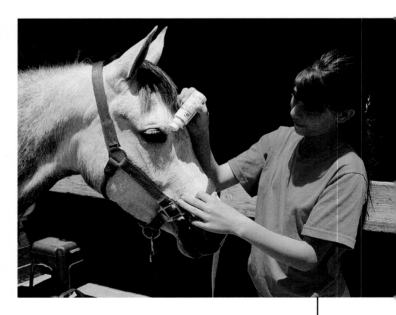

Roll-on fly sprays are handy to use around the ears and eyes.

HOOF CARE

With a hoof pick, clean your horse's hooves every day—before and after you ride. Hooves get packed with mud, or stones get wedged in hooves and make your horse lame. If you live in a wet area, his feet could also get thrush if not picked out regularly. Here's how to use a hoof pick:

1. Start with the left foreleg and face your horse's tail. Run your hand down his leg so he knows you are going to pick up his hoof.

2. He should pick up his hoof when you touch the pastern just above the hoof. If he refuses to cooperate, there are two tricks you can try. You can pinch his pastern, or you can lean against him with your shoulder until he takes the weight off the foot you want to pick up.

3. Hold the hoof in your left hand and the hoof pick in your right. Use the pointed end of the pick to remove debris. Always work from the heel (the back of the hoof) to the toe (the front). Take special care to clean out the dirt in the V-shaped groove around the frog. When you finish, put his foot down gently.

4. Pick out the rear hoof in the same way, looking backward again. Stand next to the horse, not behind him.

5. Pick out the hooves on the other side, starting with the foreleg. You can wash the outside of the hoof with a brush and water.

Pick out your horse's hooves every day.

Use the hoof pick from heel to toe.

Hoof Oil and Dressings

If you live in a dry climate, hooves may dry out and crack. For this condition, apply hoof oil or dressing to the bottom of the hoof and the hoof wall on a regular basis. Hoof oil or dressing moisturizes hooves. It also makes them shine, so people often apply it at shows to make a horse's hooves look great.

If your horse's hooves are chipping, your farrier or vet may advise you to add a special hoof supplement to his diet. You can buy this at a tack shop or feed merchant. Some supplements contain biotin, a B-complex vitamin that helps to strengthen hooves.

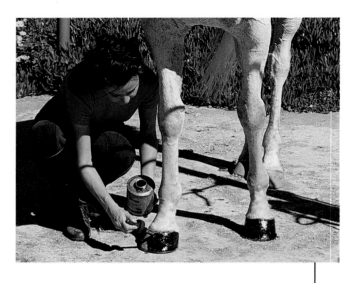

Apply oil to moisturize dry hooves.

Your horse will need a visit from the farrier every four to six weeks.

THE FARRIER

The farrier trims your horse's hooves and puts shoes on him if needed. A horse's hooves are like human nails. They grow about a quarter of an inch a month, so they need to be trimmed and filed (rasped) into shape every five to six weeks. If your horse's hooves get too long, they crack and make it difficult for him to move properly. He could also become sore and lame.

Most riding horses wear shoes made of iron, steel, or aluminum to protect their feet. Horses ridden on rocky trails, roads, or hard ground need shoes to prevent their hooves from wearing down. Shoes can also be used to prevent a horse from slipping—especially on grass—and some come with studs to give the horse better footing. Show jumpers and three-day eventers often have studs in their shoes.

If your horse has hoof problems, a farrier may make specially designed shoes to help the hooves grow normally. Special shoes are also used on horses with gait or movement problems caused by conformation defects. A skilled farrier may be able to correct a horse's movement problem.

If your horse is not ridden on hard surfaces or spends all his time in a pasture, he may not need shoes, but he still needs his hooves trimmed. Trimming is less expensive than shoeing.

Ask your instructor or a horsey friend to recommend an experienced farrier. If he has shod a horse in your barn, check out his work before you make an appointment. He will usually come to your horse. Have your horse ready and tied up, and pick out his hooves before the farrier arrives. Your horse should be used to having his hooves touched, so don't expect the farrier to train him for you.

Farriers make regular visits to big barns. If you sign up your horse, he'll locate him. All you have to do is leave a check. Make a point, however, of talking to your farrier every once in a while, especially if you have questions about your horse's hooves or the way he moves.

Be prepared to call the farrier if you notice excessive cracking or chipping, the hoof growing over the shoe, loose nails, or a loose shoe. Keep a pair of pliers or pincers (special pliers used by a farrier) in your tack box so you can pull off a loose shoe. Your farrier can show you how.

It's Shoe Time!

Get into the habit of having the farrier trim and shoe your horse every six weeks. It usually takes about an hour to an hour and a half. Here's what the farrier does:

1. Trims off the excess hoof with a hoof knife or trimmers

2. Levels the foot with a rasp (file)

3. Hammers a shoe into the shape of the hoof on an anvil. Some farriers do hot shoeing, which means they heat the shoe in a portable oven and shape it on the anvil. There are people who believe hot shoes fit the hoof better. Hot shoeing is often used if a horse needs special shoes. Cold shoeing uses ready-made shoes. The farrier can shape the shoe to a degree by hammering it on the anvil, but not as much as when hot shoeing.

4. Checks the fit of the shoe by holding it against the bottom of the hoof. If the shoe is hot, he presses it into the hoof and burns an imprint. Although the burned hoof smells a bit, the process is painless and it helps the farrier fit the shoe accurately. If it doesn't fit, he continues to shape it on the anvil.

5. Nails the shoe to the hoof. If the shoe is hot, the farrier first dips it into cool water. He hammers the nails through the shoe and into the bottom of the hoof. The sharp ends come out on the side. The farrier bends these pieces into the hoof and cuts off the points. The bent end forms a "clinch," which holds the shoe on the hoof.

6. Flattens the clinches and rasps them as smooth as possible

Occasionally, a horse is lame after being shod. This is usually caused by a nail pricking a sensitive area in the hoof. If your horse seems sore after shoeing, call your farrier and describe the lameness. He should come out and remove the shoe, and you may have to soak the hoof in Epsom salts for a few days before he can put it back on. To do this, fill a shallow soft-rubber bucket with warm water, and add about $\frac{3}{4}$ cup of Epsom salts. Stir the mixture for a moment, then place your horse's hoof in the bucket. Keep an eye on your horse, or hold him with a lead rope so you can control him if he spooks and knocks the bucket over.

Chapter Six

TACK AND GEAR

THE BRIDLE, SADDLE, AND OTHER EQUIPMENT you use on your horse are called tack. You can buy tack at a tack shop or order it from a catalog. You can also buy used tack at an auction, a horse fair, or from a private owner—be observant if you do. The tack could have loose stitching or be broken. Study it carefully before you pay for it.

English and western riding each has its own kind of tack, so buy tack for your style of riding. If you want to jump, a bulky western saddle is not for you. If you want to trail ride for hours, a flat jumping saddle won't be very comfortable. Visit a tack shop or look at a catalog with your instructor or a horsey friend, and ask them to advise you on tack. Also, check out the gear that other people at your barn are using. Here is what you need to start.

A leather halter is safer than a nylon one.

THE HALTER

A halter is a harness made of leather or strong nylon. It gives you control over your horse when you're not riding her. A halter has no bit, so you can tie her while she's wearing it. Most halters have a metal ring underneath the horse's jaw, where you clip a lead rope. Lead ropes are made of cotton or nylon.

If your horse is frisky or disobedient when you lead her, fasten a chain to the lead rope and run it over her nose. This gives you extra control, but never tie a horse using a chain because if she pulls back she could injure her face.

THE BRIDLE

A bridle is buckled over your horse's head. It can be made of leather or a synthetic material and comes in several sizes: pony, cob (a large pony or small horse), and horse. Western bridles are often called headstalls. Bridles have buckles and hooks to help you adjust them to fit your horse perfectly.

English Bridles

Almost all English or hunt-seat bridles look the same. They consist of:

A crown (or head) piece with a throat-latch attached to it

Two cheekpieces, which attach to the bit

A noseband

A browband

Reins, which attach to the bit

A bit, which goes in the horse's mouth

An English bridle with a simple cavesson noseband

A western bridle suitable for showing

REINS

Reins attach to the bit that goes in your horse's mouth. They are one or two straps that you hold in your hands. The open or split rein is a commonly used western rein. It is made of two separate straps, $\frac{3}{8}$ to 1 inch wide and about 6 to 8 feet long, with decorative braiding on the ends. The two straps are crossed over the withers. Pulling on a rein puts pressure on the bit, which then puts pressure on your horse's mouth. This pressure tells your horse to slow down, stop, or turn.

Western Bridles

Western headstalls are often flashier than their English counterparts. They may be decorated with fancy stitching, silver buckles, and silver or metal coin-size decorations called "conchas." They come in two main styles: A browband style, similar to an English bridle, and a one-ear style, which has a loop in the crown piece where the ear pokes through

Like English-style bridles, most western headstalls have a bit that is fastened to cheekpieces and reins. But most western headstalls do not have a noseband.

BITS

Bits are made of stainless steel, rubber, or nylon, and come in different sizes. If a bit is too small, it pinches and hurts your horse's mouth. If it's too big, it won't work properly.

There are hundreds of bits to choose from. Some bits are mild; others are strong and can hurt a horse's mouth—especially if a rider has rough hands. If you're just starting out or have a young horse, it's best to use a mild bit. This is usually a snaffle. If your horse is extra strong, you may need to try other bits until you find one that enables you to control your horse.

The Snaffle

Snaffle bits are used by both western and English riders. They have two rings, which attach to the bridle, and a mouthpiece, which is hinged to the rings. The mouthpiece may be unjointed (one piece) or jointed (two pieces joined in the middle). The thinner the mouthpiece, the more severe the bit. If a snaffle has a thick mouthpiece, it is probably quite mild.

Here are a few snaffles you could try on your horse:

D-Ring: A D-ring snaffle is a single-jointed bit with a rubber or metal mouthpiece. D-shaped rings at each end prevent the bit from being pulled through the horse's mouth. This is a super bit for a quiet or young horse.

Full Cheek: This bit has 4- to 5-inch-long cheekpieces that put pressure on the sides of the horse's mouth and cheek, giving the rider more steering power. If your horse is hard to turn, this is the bit for her.

Eggbutt: The rings on the side of the eggbutt bit are welded to the mouthpiece. This is a mild bit, often seen at shows on horses competing in hunter seat classes.

Unjointed: An unjointed snaffle is made of rubber and is very mild. It is often used on young horses. It is sometimes called a "dog bone bit."

Loose Ring (sometimes called an O-ring by western riders): The rings on the sides of this mild bit are not fixed to the mouthpiece. This lets the mouthpiece move around in a horse's mouth. Many horses play with their mouthpieces, which produces saliva that keeps their mouths soft and responsive to the bit. A loose ring snaffle is often used on youngsters and dressage horses.

Twisted: This severe snaffle has a twisted mouthpiece, and when you pull on the reins, it feels rough against the horse's mouth. When she slows down, relieve the pressure in her mouth by softening your hold on the reins. This bit is often used on strong horses who pull a lot.
If you can't stop or control your horse effectively in a snaffle, try another type of bit.

An eggbutt snaffle

An unjointed snaffle

Curb Bits

Many English and western riders use bits from the curb family. A curb bit (often called a "shank bit" by western riders) encourages a horse to lower her head, which makes the bit work more effectively. Curb bits are usually shaped like a capital H. They have long cheekpieces and an unjointed mouthpiece.

Curb bits work by leverage. When pressure from your hand is applied to a rein (attached to a ring on the bottom of the bit), the top of the bit moves forward pulling the bridle down so it presses on your horse's poll. She then lowers her head.

Curb bits have a small chain that goes under the horse's jaw. When you pull on the reins, the chain presses on the horse's jaw and encourages her to flex more. Here are some popular curb bits:

The Basic Curb Bit: Used by most western riders, this bit is made of metal and is usually unjointed. Most western curbs have a raised port—a bump in the middle of the mouthpiece. The port puts extra pressure on a horse's tongue and mouth. Some western riders have beautiful curb bits with cheekpieces engraved or overlaid with silver.

The Pelham: This unjointed bit uses two reins and a curb chain. The top rein attaches to the big ring (the snaffle ring) on the cheekpiece. When you pull on this rein, the bit acts like a snaffle. The second rein fastens to the small bottom ring (the curb ring). When you pull on this rein, it puts pressure on the horse's mouth and poll. Pelhams have rubber or metal mouthpieces.

Holding two reins can be difficult, so many riders use a "bit converter"—a leather strap that attaches to both the snaffle and curb rings so you can use one rein. A bit converter makes a Pelham work like a strong snaffle.

A western curb bit

A pelham

Gag Bits

Gag bits raise up the head and are used on horses who put their heads down and take off with their riders! Once a horse's head is up, it's easier for a rider to stop her. Gag bits are very strong and should not be used by novices.

Some western riders use a full-cheek gag that looks similar to a curb bit. It can be jointed or unjointed. When the rein is pulled, the mouthpiece slides up the long cheekpieces and puts pressure on a horse's mouth. You may spot western gags in timed events in which a horse has to stop and turn quickly.

HACKAMORES

Hackamores are bitless bridles used on horses who dislike bits. A hackamore has reins attached to a noseband. When you pull on the reins, the noseband puts pressure on the horse's nose. A hackamore can cause pain and affect a horse's breathing, so use it gently.

A mechanical hackamore has a noseband with metal cheekpieces. It works like a curb bit, putting pressure on a horse's poll. A bosal hackamore has a simple noseband made of leather or rope, and puts pressure on a horse's nose and jaw.

A western bosal hackamore

NOSEBANDS

Nosebands are part of an English bridle, and there are different types, each with its own use. You may need to try a few before you find one that suits your horse. Here are a few popular nosebands:

Cavesson: This is the simplest noseband. It fastens below the cheekbone and above the bit.

Dropped Noseband: This fastens under the bit and prevents a horse from opening her mouth and avoiding the bit. It can interfere with her breathing if not fitted properly. Only use it with a snaffle, never with a curb bit or gag.

Flash Noseband: This has a thin leather strap that threads through a loop on the front of the noseband. The strap fastens below the bit and stops a horse from opening her mouth.

MARTINGALES

Martingales are leather straps that keep a horse from throwing her head up to avoid the bit. There are two kinds:

Running Martingale: A running martingale has a leather strap that runs from the girth and divides into two thinner straps with metal rings on the ends. The reins are threaded through these rings. When your horse puts her head up high, a running martingale puts pressure on the bit though the reins.

A Standing Martingale or Western Tie-Down: This is a single leather strap that runs from the girth, between the forelegs, to the underside of the noseband. It is kept in place by a separate neck strap. Standing martingales and tie-downs put pressure on a horse's nose and are only used with a plain noseband. Often a tie-down or a standing martingale is fastened to a breastplate.

BREASTPLATE, OR WESTERN BREAST COLLAR

Sometimes saddles move around or slip back. If a horse has low withers, for example, the saddle may slide from side to side. A breastplate/breast collar helps keep it secure.

A breastplate is a leather strap loosely worn across a horse's chest and attached to D-rings on the front of the saddle and the girth. They are often used by people who jump cross-country, such as eventers and hunting folk, or by people who trail ride through mountainous terrain.

A bridle with a flash noseband

A running martingale

THE SADDLE

A saddle is your seat on a horse. It helps you keep your balance so you don't interfere with your horse's natural movement.

The type of saddle you use depends on the kind of riding you do. There are English saddles for jumping, dressage, and eventing. There are western saddles for trail riding and roping calves. There are endurance saddles for long, competitive rides.

You must buy a saddle that fits both you and your horse. Ask your instructor to inspect the saddle and watch you ride in it. It has to be comfortable because you'll be spending a lot of time in it. Most tack stores let you take a saddle on a trial basis for a day or two. You'll have to pay for the saddle, but if you bring it back in pristine condition, the store should give you your money back. Check the store's return policy before taking a saddle.

The foundation of a saddle is the tree, a wooden or fiberglass frame that is reinforced with metal and covered in padding and leather or a synthetic material. Leather is more traditional, but synthetic saddles tend to be lighter and easier to clean. On an English saddle, the stirrup bars, the metal strips around which you loop the stirrup leathers, are attached to the tree. On a western saddle, the tops of the stirrup fenders loop through a slot on both sides of the tree.

A standing martingale

English and western saddles are different in basic design.

English Saddles

There are several types of English saddle:

General Purpose Saddle: If you are going to be doing a little bit of everything, buy a GP saddle. It usually has thigh and knee rolls to keep your legs in the correct position, and its panels and flaps are cut slightly forward in case you do some jumping.

Show Jumping Saddle: This saddle is designed to bring the rider forward and off the horse's back as the horse jumps a fence. Show jumpers tend to ride with short stirrups, so the saddle flaps are cut forward and provide plenty of room for the rider's knees.

Dressage Saddle: This saddle lets the rider's seat and legs have a lot of contact with the horse. The rider must sit up straight, so a dressage saddle has a deep seat. It also has long, straight flaps that don't interfere with a rider's leg position.

Dressage saddles have deep seats and long flaps.

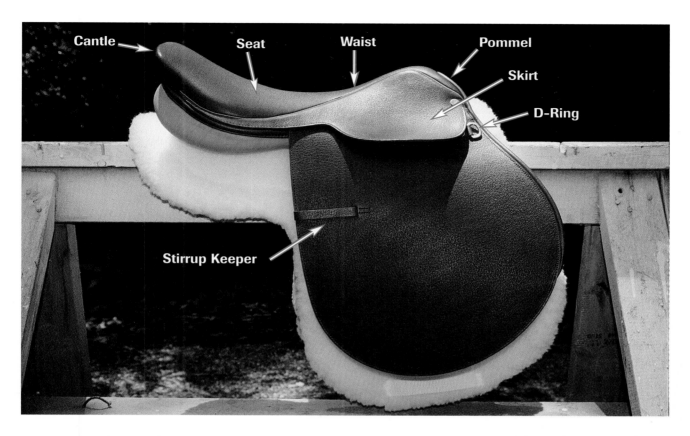

Cantle

Seat

Waist

Pommel

Skirt

D-Ring

Stirrup Keeper

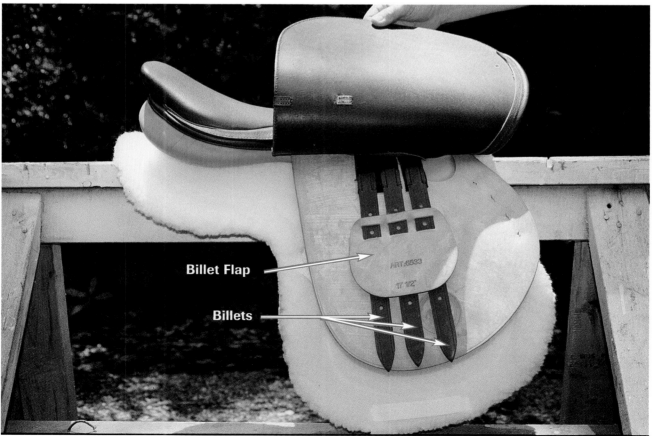

Billet Flap

Billets

Western saddles

Western saddles are bigger and heavier than English saddles. They can weigh more than 30 pounds. They have wider seats for comfort on long rides. They spread a rider's weight more evenly on a horse's back than an English saddle.

The most distinguishing feature of the western saddle is the protruding horn in the front. Working cowboys and show or rodeo competitors use it to rope cows and horses. The horn also comes in handy for new riders to hold onto in emergencies, but don't get into the habit of holding onto the horn. Not only will you look like a beginner, but it also throws off your balance. If you need extra stability, hold onto the cantle (back of the seat). Instead of pulling you forward, this keeps you deep in the seat.

Western saddles come in different styles.

General Purpose Saddle: The most commonly used western saddle is the General Purpose Saddle. It is popular with pleasure riders and folk who enjoy trail riding. It features a deep seat padded for extra comfort. It has a small horn because pleasure riders don't often rope calves!

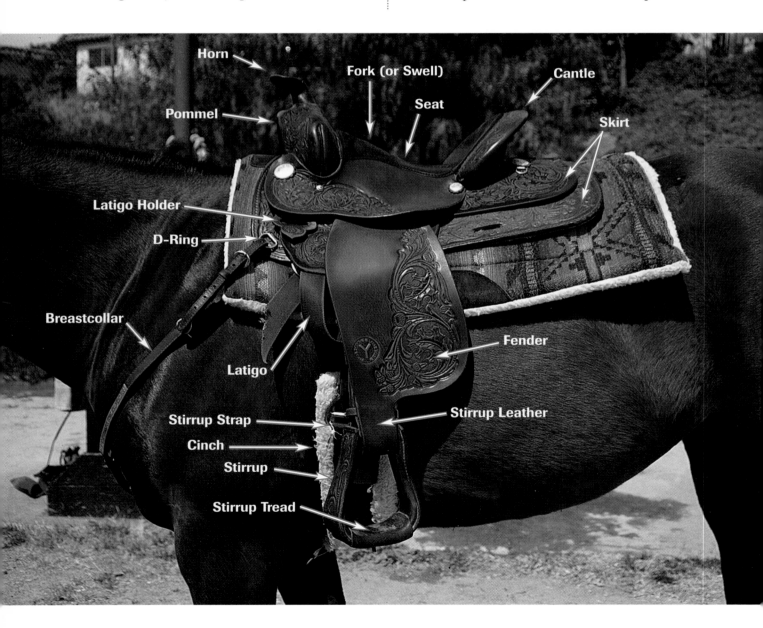

Equitation Saddle: This is designed for show. The leather is often elaborately decorated with intricate embossing or hand-tooled designs. It is used in equitation classes and parades. The horn is fairly small. The seat is padded and is usually covered in suede to help the rider stick in the saddle.

Roping Saddle: A roping saddle is a heavy-duty saddle made of tough leather. The horn is large because riders use it to rope cows or store their coiled lassos. A roping saddle usually has a flat seat and a low cantle so a rider can hop in and out quickly and easily while he or she is working.

SADDLE-RELATED TACK
Saddle Pad

When you ride, a pad goes under your saddle to keep it clean and protect your horse's back. Saddle pads can be made of cotton, wool, fleece, felt, or foam. They are usually square or saddle-shaped, and come in a lot of colors—but white is used in the English show arena.

Western riders often use Navajo blankets—thick, rectangular pads made of wool or cotton. These colorful pads can be seen in the western show arena.

No matter what type of saddle pad you use, wash it regularly. A dirty rug rubs a horse and makes her uncomfortable. If you don't have access to a full-size washing machine (laundromats often frown on people washing hairy horse pads in their machines), then try your local tack store. Some of them provide this laundering service.

Girth or Cinch

A girth or a cinch is a belt that goes under your horse's belly and holds the saddle in place. English girths have two buckles at each end that attach to saddle girth straps. English girths are usually made of leather, thick string, or synthetic materials such as nylon.

Western girths are called cinches. They can be made of leather, mohair, cotton, wool, or synthetic materials. They have big rings at each end, one of which has a buckle tongue. Some western saddles use a rear cinch to help stabilize a saddle for roping.

Stirrup Leathers

Used on English saddles, these are long straps, with buckles, that fasten to the saddle's stirrup bar and hold the stirrup irons. Stirrup leathers suffer a lot of stress so check them for wear and tear regularly.

Fenders

The fender is the western equivalent of a stirrup leather. The fender is a wide leather strap that connects the stirrup to the saddle.

Stirrup Irons and Treads

These are footrests that attach to the saddle with stirrup leathers. English stirrups are made of steel and should have rubber treads on them to keep your feet from slipping. Western stirrups are made of wood or synthetic materials covered in leather.

BOOTS AND BANDAGES

Boots protect a horse's legs from knocks during such activities as jumping, barrel racing, and riding cross-country. Boots also help to support leg muscles because twisting a leg the wrong way—or knocking a jump—can pull, strain, or injure delicate tendons. Some horses, especially clumsy young ones or ones with poor conformation, kick themselves by mistake; in these instances, boots can help prevent injury.

Boots are made of leather or synthetic materials. They usually fasten by buckles or Velcro straps. The most commonly used boots are brushing boots, fetlock or ankle boots, and over-reach boots, also called bell boots.

Brushing boots, sometimes called splint boots, have padding that covers the inside of the leg, and protect a horse if she hits the inside of one leg with the opposite hoof. They can be used on all four legs and cover the lower leg only.

Fetlock or ankle boots are a short version of the brushing boot and are used for the same purpose. They cover the fetlock and heel area.

Over-reach boots, or bell boots, belong on the front hooves. They fit around the pastern and protect the heels and coronet. Usually made of rubber and bell-shaped, they may fasten with buckles or Velcro—or simply pull over the hoof. When a horse jumps or gallops, a back hoof may knock a front hoof, injuring the pastern or the heel, or it may pull off a front shoe. Over-reach boots help to prevent these things from happening.

Exercise bandages also give support and protect a horse's leg from knocks and bumps. They cover the lower leg, from just below the knee to just above the fetlock. Exercise bandages are made of a stretchy material and usually have Velcro fastenings or ties to secure them. They should be put on over some sort of padding.

Bandages must be put on correctly in order to work. If you are new to riding, it's better to use boots. Bandages that are too tight interfere with blood circulation and can damage tendons. If they're too loose, they may unravel and trip your horse. Have an experienced horse person show you how to put them on.

These brushing boots and over-reach boots are being used together.

BLANKETS

A blanket keeps a horse warm in chilly weather, dry in rain, and cools her down and dries her off if she is sweaty. Clipped horses have to wear blankets.

When you shop for a blanket, buy the correct size. Too small and it will be uncomfortable, too big and it may rub your horse and cause ugly sores. To get an approximate blanket size, take a tape measure and measure her from the middle of her chest to the middle of her hindquarters. Check the fit before you remove the tags. You should be able to put your hand comfortably all around the neck opening, and there should be room between the horse's belly and the straps.

Here are the most commonly used blankets:

Antisweat Sheet: A cotton web mesh sheet that is full of holes, which allow air to circulate near a horse's sweaty skin, letting her dry off more quickly. An antisweat sheet works best if used under a stable sheet or blanket.

Cooler: An extra-long acrylic or wool blanket used on a sweaty, hot horse. It cools her down, absorbs dampness, and prevents chills. It covers a horse's neck and goes down to her knees. It has a strap that goes in front of her ears to keep it in place.

New Zealand Rug: A super tough turn-out blanket made of heavyweight, waterproof canvas. It is used in very cold or wet places.

Stable Blanket: If your horse is clipped, she must wear a blanket in her stable. Stable blankets usually have a nylon shell with padded insulation underneath.

Stable or Show Sheet: Your horse may lie down in the stable and get covered in manure. Lightweight stable or show sheets keep her clean. They are made of nylon, polyester, or cotton, and have no padding.

Turn-Out Blanket: Your horse should be turned out every day. If the weather is cold and your horse is clipped—or has a thin coat—she should wear a turn-out blanket of strong nylon to repel rain. The inside of the blanket should have a woolen or an acrylic lining.

All blankets need to be cleaned. Throw yours into a washing machine at least twice a month or it will get covered in smelly stains. A New Zealand rug won't fit in a washer, so every three months you should hose it down and give it a scrub with a brush and warm water. Then, when it's dry, treat it with a waterproofing spray or paint you can buy at a tack shop.

A stable blanket

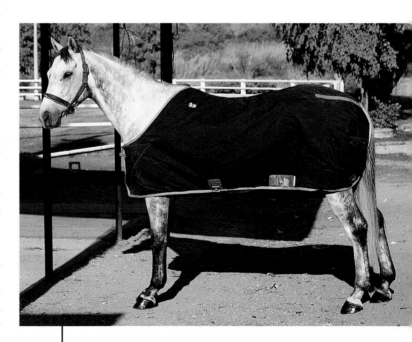

A turn-out sheet

Tacking Up Your Horse

TACKING UP YOUR HORSE SEEMS COMPLICATED at first because there are a lot of confusing straps and buckles. Don't be afraid to ask for help. If you take riding lessons, watch a groom get your horse ready a few times; then ask to tack him up yourself. This is the best way to learn.

CARRYING TACK

When you carry tack, it's best to hang the bridle over your shoulder. Rest an English saddle and pad on your forearm, and lay the girth over the saddle. Western folk grab the cantle with their right hand and hold on to the front of the saddle—not the horn—with their left.

If you must put a saddle on the ground, set it on its front end with the back end leaning against a wall or fence post. Drape the girth or cinch between the saddle and the wall so the saddle doesn't get scratched.

The correct way to carry English tack.

TACKING UP
ENGLISH STYLE

1. Fasten the pad to the saddle by its straps. Stand on your horse's left side and lightly place the saddle and pad in front of his withers (too far forward), then gently slide them back into their correct position. This keeps the hair under the saddle smooth. Ruffled hair causes friction under the saddle, which can irritate a horse.

2. Walk around to your horse's right side with the girth, and attach it to the girth straps. Most people use the two outside straps. (The extra strap is there in case one breaks.) Now, go to the left side, pull the girth underneath your horse's belly, and attach it to the two outside straps. Don't tighten it right away. Do it gradually, then pull the buckle guard down over the buckles.

3. Make sure the saddle pad is pulled up into the gullet (the long tunnel under the saddle), so it doesn't put pressure on your horse's spine.

Slide an English saddle back into place.

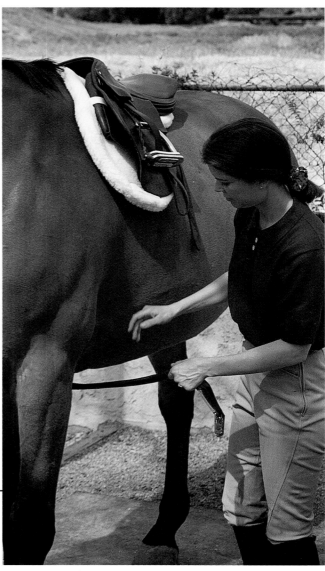

Bring the girth up slowly so you don't scare your horse.

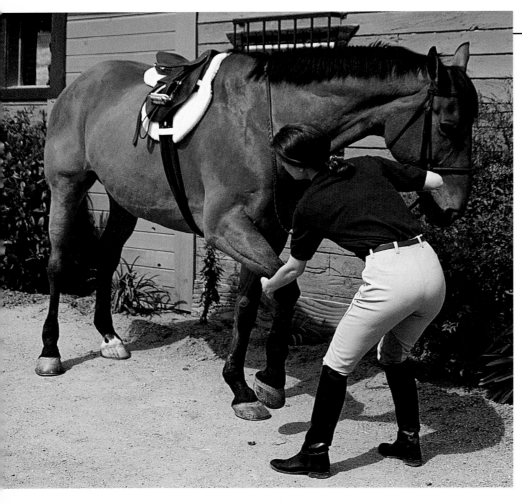

Stretch out the front legs so the girth doesn't pinch skin.

4. After you tighten the girth for the last time, and before you mount, stretch out your horse's forelegs to make sure the skin under the girth is smooth. Wrinkled skin causes sores.

5. Now to the bridle. Hold it in front of your horse's head, and slip the reins over his head so you have some control when you take off the halter.

Put the reins over your horse's head first.

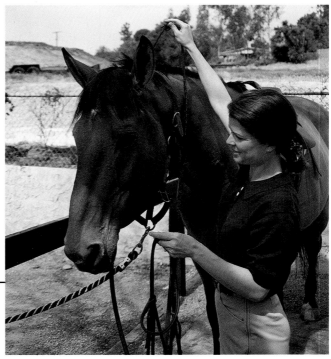

Gently slide the bit into your horse's mouth.

6. Stand next to your horse and take off his halter. Quickly slip your right hand under his neck and take hold of the bridle's cheekpieces. Your right hand should keep his head down. Put your left hand underneath the bit and bring it gently between his lips and up into his mouth. Your right hand should lift the bridle so the bit slips into place. Adjust the noseband so it's in the correct place and fasten it.

7. Once the bit is in place, hold the crown piece in your left hand. Use your right hand to gently bring his left ear, and then his right ear, under the crown piece. Straighten it out behind his ears.

8. Loosely fasten the throatlatch under his jaw. You should be able to fit four fingers between it and his throat.

9. Secure all the loose ends of straps in their leather keepers.

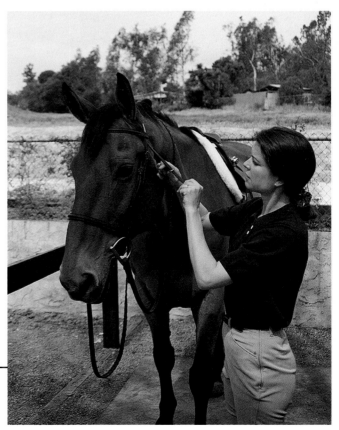

Fasten the throatlatch last.

TACKING UP
WESTERN STYLE

1. Check your blanket for twigs or burrs that could irritate your horse's skin. Place the blanket on the horse's back, slightly forward, then slide it back into position. Make sure it hangs evenly on both sides of your horse.

2. Pick up the saddle by the horn, and then hold the front of the saddle with your left hand partially in the gullet. Your right hand can hold the back of the saddle. Place the right stirrup and cinch over the seat of the saddle so they don't bang your horse when you place the saddle on his back.

Stand on your horse's left side and swing the saddle into position on your horse's back. Do it swiftly, but gently. Western saddles are heavy, and you may hurt your horse's back or scare him if you slam the saddle in place.

3. Walk around to the other side and lower the stirrups and cinch. Check that nothing is twisted. Release any saddle strings that might be stuck under the saddle. Return to the left side and make sure the saddle is sitting correctly. If it looks out of kilter, grab the horn and gently shake the saddle until it slips into place.

4. Stick a couple of fingers under the saddle pad right over the withers and lift it up a bit into the gullet.

Swing a western saddle into place.

Do up the cinch slowly.

5. Put up your left stirrup and reach underneath your horse for the cinch. Put the long latigo in your right hand and then run it down and up through the cinch ring. If the saddle is in the correct place, the cinch should be about 4 inches away from your horse's elbow. Then tighten the latigo. If you have a cinch with a buckle, simply buckle it to the latigo. If it is a traditional cinch without a buckle, tie the latigo to it with a knot.

6. If your saddle has a rear cinch, fasten it next. It shouldn't be as tight as the front one. Now connect the strap from the back cinch to the front cinch. Slip the excess latigo through the latigo holder.

Carefully slide the crown piece over your horse's ears.

7. If you use a breastplate, put it on now. It shouldn't be so tight that it presses on your horse's windpipe.

8. Unbuckle your horse's halter and rebuckle it around his neck so he can't move off.

9. Stand next to your horse, facing the same direction he faces. Hold the crown piece with your right hand and separate the bit from the curb chain with your left. Gently slip the bit into the horse's mouth. If your horse won't open his mouth, sticking your thumb into the corner of his mouth may make him open up.

10. As the bit slides in, raise the crown piece and carefully slide it over the left ear. Then, hold the crown piece in your left hand and use your right hand to slip his right ear under the crown piece or into its ear slot.

DOES YOUR TACK FIT?

It's important that your tack fits your horse. If it's too big, it can rub and cause sores. If it's too small, it can pinch and make him uncomfortable. Here are some ways to make sure it fits properly:

When you're in the saddle, you should be able to fit at least three fingers between the front of the saddle and the withers.

The saddle's gullet should be wide enough to clear your horse's spine.

If you have an English saddle, you should be able to fit three fingers between the cantle and your horse's back. If you have a western saddle, you should be able to fit three fingers between the back of the skirt and your horse's back.

🐎 The stuffing or fleece on the bottom of the saddle should be smooth and without lumps so there is even pressure on your horse's back.

🐎 Above the bit, there should be two or three wrinkles in the skin around the corner of his mouth. If there are no wrinkles, the bit may be too low in his mouth.

🐎 Check that the curb chain fits properly. You should be able to fit two fingers between the chain and the chin.

🐎 Make sure the western cinch rings are even on both sides of the horse.

You should be able to fit at least three fingers in an English saddle's gullet.

UNTACKING ENGLISH STYLE

1. First, take off the bridle. Unfasten the noseband and the throatlatch.

2. Slip the crown piece over your horse's ears with your right hand, and lower the bridle so that the bit comes out of his mouth. Do it slowly so the bit doesn't bang his teeth. Keep the reins over his neck for control.

3. Put on your horse's halter and lead rope, then lift the reins over his head.

4. Run the irons up the leather until they are near the stirrup bars. Secure them by threading the rest of the leather through the stirrup.

5. Unbuckle the girth on the left side of your horse. Next, lift the saddle and pad off together. If the pad is damp, remove it and hang it up to dry.

UNTACKING WESTERN STYLE

1. Take off the bridle first. Leave the reins over the horse's neck. Unfasten the throatlatch if there is one.

2. Bring the crown piece over the ears with your right hand, and slowly lower the bridle so the bit comes out of his mouth without banging his teeth. Put on his halter and lift the reins over his head.

3. If your saddle has a rear cinch, unfasten it first. Then unfasten the front cinch.

4. Secure the cinches and stirrups over the saddle so they don't swing.

5. Grab the front and back of the saddle, lift, and swing it off.

CLEANING YOUR TACK

Rinse off your bit after every ride, and clean your tack at least once a week. Saddlery is expensive, and it will last longer if you keep it clean. Dirty tack becomes stiff and breaks. When you clean your tack, check that the stitching isn't coming undone. If it's loose, take it to a tack shop for repair.

Things You Need for Cleaning Tack

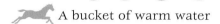 A bucket of warm water

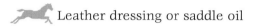 Leather dressing or saddle oil

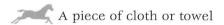 A piece of cloth or towel

 Saddle soap

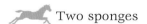 Two sponges

Cleaning Tack, Step by Step

1. Take apart the bridle, piece by piece. Remove the stirrups and leathers from the saddle.

2. Dunk the bit in the bucket to soak. Then clean it off, rinse it, and leave it to dry. Your stirrups can go in the bucket next.

3. Dip one sponge in the water and wring it. It should be damp—not soaking wet. Use this sponge to clean your saddle and bridle, piece by piece.

4. When the leather is dry, put some saddle oil or dressing on a rag and work it into the areas of your tack that get used a lot, for example inside grooves and folds. Give the oil time to soak in.

5. Dampen the other sponge slightly. Rub or spray saddle soap on it and work it into the leather. Saddle soap gives your tack a protective coat and makes it shiny.

6. Finally, take a cloth and polish your saddle and bridle.

A coating of saddle soap protects leather.

Tack that gets a lot of wear needs to be oiled frequently.

TRAILERING A HORSE

IF YOU PLAN TO TAKE YOUR HORSE TO SHOWS, other events, or on trail rides more than a few miles from her home, you will have to load her into a trailer and drive there. But don't dash out and buy a trailer right away. If you take lessons, your instructor may organize trailering for her students. She may get a big rig and share the costs or include them in the overall price of the outing. You might also find someone with a

trailer who would like company going to horse events. Offer to share expenses and help pay for gas.

If you decide to buy a trailer, first make sure you have a vehicle that can pull it. Most experts recommend towing with a truck or utility vehicle that has a V-8 engine and a special towing package. If you plan to tow only one horse or are considering a lightweight trailer,

Make sure your vehicle is powerful enough to pull a trailer.

you may be able to pull with a V-6, but in either case, invest in a solid third-class hitch, which is safer and stronger than a bumper pull.

WHAT KIND OF TRAILER DO YOU NEED?

Trailers come with either a ramp or a step-up entrance. Everyone has a preference. If you have no problems loading your horse, a step-up trailer may suit you fine, but some horses prefer getting in and out of a trailer using a ramp. Before you buy a trailer, try loading your horse into both types. Consider her reactions when you are shopping. Trailers with ramps tend to be heavier than the step-up types, so you must think about this if you have a small towing vehicle.

Some trailers carry the horses facing forward, side by side; others carry them at a slant. Slant trailers are sometimes called stock trailers; they usually carry three or more horses. Many people feel that horses balance themselves better when they travel at an angle. One type to avoid is the one-horse trailer. These can become unbalanced and tip over. It's better to spend the extra money and buy a more secure two-horse trailer.

Some two-horse trailers have mangers with storage space underneath for tack. Those without storage space are called "walk-throughs" because you can lead your horse into the trailer, duck under a breast bar, and stand up again in an empty area. Most of these have small escape doors at the front. Some trailers have dressing rooms too.

A horse who is easy to load won't mind stepping up into the trailer.

Some horses find walking up a ramp easier than stepping up into a trailer.

If you plan to do a lot of towing and have a big, tough truck, you could buy a gooseneck trailer. A gooseneck fastens to a hitch in the truckbed and balances its load over the back axle of the truck. Goosenecks give a horse a smoother ride than some other types of trailers.

American trailers generally come in four sizes: pony, quarter horse, Thoroughbred, and warmblood. Measure your horse before you start shopping. She needs plenty of headroom in her trailer.

LOOKING FOR A TRAILER

If you have the money and want to buy a brand-new trailer, check the *Yellow Pages* in your phone book and local horse magazines for a dealer. But if money is tight, look for a used trailer in the Classified Ads of a local horse magazine or newspaper. Here are some things to check before handing over any money for a used trailer:

Flooring: Lift up mats and look underneath the trailer to make sure the floor wood is strong, not rotting or weak.

Brakes: Most trailers have electrical brakes. Make sure they work!

Lights: Test all the lights.

Windows: A trailer needs windows for ventilation.

Rust: If a trailer has a lot of rust, pass it by!

Chains: These hold the trailer to the truck if the hitch comes undone.

Tires, Ramp, Partition, and Axle: Check for wear and tear.

TRAVELING GEAR

Because traveling in a trailer is bumpy, a horse must wear protective gear to prevent injuries. Here's what you need:

Shipping Boots: These are padded boots that fasten easily with Velcro straps and are sold in sets of four. The best boots cover the knees and hooves of a horse's forelegs and the hocks and hooves of her hind legs. They are easy to put on and remove.

Always put shipping boots on your horse's legs before a trip.

Shipping Bandages: Some people use bandages made of stretchy fabric instead of boots, but they must have some sort of padding under them or they won't offer protection. They take longer than boots to put on and remove.

Head Bumper: If your horse throws her head around in a trailer, she should wear a head bumper. This is a padded hat with ear holes that attaches to the halter.

Tail Bandage: Some horses rub their tails on the back of a trailer. A stretchy tail bandage keeps the tail tidy and clean. It wraps around the top of a horse's tail and usually stops halfway down, where the tailbone ends.

For emergencies, always carry an extra halter and lead rope, plus a lead shank.

A head bumper

LOADING A HORSE

Before loading your horse, make the trailer as comfortable and pleasant as possible. Put straw or sawdust on the floor and make sure it's free of any slippery stuff, such as manure. Hang hay in a net or place it in the manger so your horse has something to nibble on during the journey. Open the escape doors so the trailer is full of light and not scary. Finally, lower the ramp or open the doors.

There are two ways of loading your horse depending on whether you have a walk-through or step-up trailer. Before loading either type of trailer, check that your horse's traveling boots or bandages are secure and that all straps are fastened properly. If your horse can be naughty put a chain over her nose.

If you have a walk-through trailer or a big stock trailer with plenty of room and your horse is quiet and well behaved, you can lead her into the trailer. Walk next to her as you approach the trailer, then take a step or two in front of her. Walk briskly up the ramp or step. Your horse should follow. If you have a walk-through, you can duck under the breast bar so you don't get run over. Tie your horse to a piece of safety string attached to the tie-up ring.

If you have a step-up trailer or a horse who doesn't load easily, drape the lead rope over her neck and tie it to itself underneath so it doesn't drag on the floor or get caught on something. Hold the lead rope a couple of inches under the horse's halter and walk along beside her, as you would normally. When you reach the trailer, turn so you are facing her shoulder. Give her a verbal signal or tap her gently with a long dressage crop or lunge whip on her hindquarters and ask her to move forward, as if she were on a lunge line. Let go of the lead rope. Give her a pat on her rear to reassure her as she steps up.

Drape the lead rope over your horse's neck when loading.

Sometimes the tap of a whip is needed to persuade a horse to load.

Once your horse is in the trailer, stand to one side and fasten the butt bar or chain as quickly as possible. Never stand directly behind her in case she steps back and stomps on you by mistake. Then, if the trailer has a ramp, lift it up, and secure all of the doors. Finally, walk to the front of the trailer, and tie your horse's lead rope to a safety string attached to a metal loop or a special stretchy trailer tie.

DRIVING A TRAILER

Driving a trailer takes practice, so go a few places without your horse first. You'll soon notice that it takes longer for your truck to stop and slow down when it's pulling several thousand pounds.

It isn't easy for a horse to stay balanced in a trailer, so you must make stops gradually and go slow and wide around corners. If you zip sharply around bends, your horse could fall down. A horse will remember a bad ride, and you may have trouble loading her next time.

UNLOADING A HORSE

Always untie your horse before unloading. If you are by yourself, open the escape door and drape the lead rope over her neck. Then head to the back of the trailer, open the door, and undo the butt bar or chain. Stand to one side and give your horse a verbal signal or gently tug on her tail to ask her to back out. Talk to her soothingly and praise her when she steps out nicely. Grab hold of the lead rope as soon as you can reach it.

Trailering Tips

🐎 Don't tie your horse too loose. She should not be able to reach over and nip at any companions.

🐎 Always load a single horse on the left side, behind the driver. Roads are convex, with the highest part being in the middle. A trailer will stay better balanced if the horse is on the left. If you are towing two horses, put the heaviest on the left.

🐎 Never get angry if you are having loading problems. Stay calm and don't upset your horse more. Ask a friend to walk behind your horse with a crop or lunge whip. He or she should give your horse a couple of light taps to make her go forward. If you are having serious problems, ask a trainer for some professional help.

🐎 Clean out the trailer immediately after every journey. Urine and manure can soak through mats and ruin a floor.

🐎 Make sure you always have a spare tire, a jack, and a lug wrench before you set off on a journey, and check your tire pressure frequently.

🐎 If going in the trailer stresses your horse, feed her in it every once in a while without driving anywhere so she gets used to being in it.

Always clean out the trailer after using it.

A CARING RELATIONSHIP

Now that you've reached the end of this book, you should have a basic knowledge of what it takes to keep a horse in your care healthy and happy. You'll know when your horse is in good health and full of vigor. On the other hand, you'll be able to spot the warning signs that tell you that your horse is feeling under the weather so you'll know when to call the veterinarian. Your feed room will be stocked with the most nutritious feed you can find so that your horse's delicate digestion system stays on an even keel. Your grooming kit will be full of the brushes, combs, and sponges needed to keep your horse sparkling clean. And your horse's tack will fit her properly and be appropriate for the type of activity you plan to enjoy with her. Because you are a knowledgeable owner, your horse is in good hands.

So, keep this book on a shelf in the barn. You may need to refer back to it from time to time. Now go out and spend some quality time with your horse!

Appendix

Useful Addresses

AMERICAN ASSOCIATION OF EQUINE PRACTITIONERS
4075 Iron Works Pike
Lexington, KY 40511-8434
606-233-0147

AMERICAN CONNEMARA PONY SOCIETY
2630 Hunting Ridge Road
Winchester, VA 22603
540-662-5953

AMERICAN DRIVING SOCIETY
PO Box 160
Metamora, MI 48455-0160
810-664-8666

AMERICAN ENDURANCE RIDE CONFERENCE
701 High Street #203
Auburn, CA 95603-4727
916-823-2260

AMERICAN FARRIERS ASSOCIATION
4059 Iron Works Pike
Lexington, KY 40511-8434
606-233-7411

AMERICAN HANOVERIAN SOCIETY
4059 Iron Works Pike
Building C
Lexington, KY 40511
606-255-4141

AMERICAN HOLSTEINER HORSE ASSOCIATION
222 E. Main Street #1
Georgetown, KY 40324-1712
502-863-4239

AMERICAN HORSE COUNCIL
1700 K Street NW
Suite 300
Washington, DC 20006-3805
202-296-4031

AMERICAN HORSE PROTECTION ASSOCIATION
1000 29th Street #T-100
Washington, DC 20007-3820
202-965-0500

AMERICAN HORSE SHOWS ASSOCIATION
220 East 42nd Street
Suite 409
New York, NY 10017
212-972-2472

AMERICAN MORGAN HORSE ASSOCIATION
PO Box 960
Shelburne, VT 05482-0960
802-985-4944

AMERICAN MUSTANG AND BURRO ASSOCIATION
PO Box 788
Lincoln, CA 95648
916-633-9271

AMERICAN PAINT HORSE ASSOCIATION
PO Box 961023
Fort Worth, TX 76161-0023
817-439-3400

AMERICAN QUARTER HORSE ASSOCIATION
PO Box 200
Amarillo, TX 79168-0001
806-376-4811

AMERICAN RIDING INSTRUCTORS ASSOCIATION (ARIA)
PO Box 282
Alton Bay, NH 03810-0282
603-875-4000

AMERICAN SADDLEBRED HORSE ASSOCIATION
4093 Iron Works Pike
Lexington, KY 40511-8434
606-259-2742

AMERICAN TRAILS
1420 E. 6th Avenue
Helena, MT 59620
406-444-4585

AMERICAN TRAKEHNER ASSOCIATION
1520 West Church Street
Newark, OH 43055
614-344-1111

AMERICAN WARMBLOOD SOCIETY
6801 W. Romley Avenue
Phoenix, AZ 85043
602-936-6621

AMERICAN YOUTH HORSE COUNCIL
4193 Iron Works Pike
Lexington, KY 40511-2742
800-TRY-AYHC

APPALOOSA HORSE CLUB, INC.
PO Box 8403
Moscow, ID 83843-0903
208-882-5578

ARABIAN HORSE REGISTRY OF AMERICA
12000 Zuni Street
Westminster, CO 80234-2300
303-450-4748

THE BUREAU OF LIVESTOCK IDENTIFICATION
1220 N Street
Sacramento, CA 95814
916-654-0889

CHA—THE ASSOCIATION FOR HORSEMANSHIP SAFETY AND EDUCATION
5318 Old Bullard Road
Tyler, TX 75703
800-399-0138

INTERCOLLEGIATE HORSE SHOW ASSOCIATION
PO Box 741
Stonybrook, NY 11790-0741
516-751-2803

INTERNATIONAL ARABIAN HORSE ASSOCIATION
Half Arabian and Anglo-Arabian Registries
PO Box 33696
Denver, CO 80233-0696
303-450-4774

THE JOCKEY CLUB
821 Corporate Drive
Lexington, KY 40503-2794
800-444-8521

NATIONAL CUTTING HORSE ASSOCIATION
4704 Hwy 377 S.
Fort Worth, TX 76116-8805
817-244-6188

NATIONAL 4-H COUNCIL
7100 Connecticut Avenue
Chevy Chase, MD 20815-4999
301-961-2959

NATIONAL HUNTER AND JUMPER ASSOCIATION
PO Box 1015
Riverside, CT 06878-1015
203-869-1225

NATIONAL REINING HORSE ASSOCIATION
448 Main Street #204
Coshocton, OH 43812-1200
614-623-0055

NORTH AMERICAN RIDING FOR THE HANDICAPPED ASSOCIATION
PO Box 33150
Denver, CO 80233
303-452-1212

PALOMINO HORSE BREEDERS OF AMERICA
15253 East Skelly Drive
Tulsa, OK 74116-2637
918-438-1234

PERFORMANCE HORSE REGISTRY
PO Box 24710
Lexington, KY 40524-4710
606-224-2880

SWEDISH WARMBLOOD ASSOCIATION OF NORTH AMERICA
PO Box 1587
Coupeville, WA 98239-1587
206-678-3503

TENNESSEE WALKING HORSE BREEDERS' AND EXHIBITORS' ASSOCIATION
PO Box 286
Lewisburg, TN 37091-0286
615-359-1574

TRAIL RIDERS OF TODAY
PO Box 30033
Bethesda, MD 20824-0033
301-854-3467

UNITED STATES COMBINED TRAINING ASSOCIATION
PO Box 2247
Leesburg, VA 22075-2247
703-779-0440

UNITED STATES DRESSAGE FEDERATION
PO Box 6669
Lincoln, NE 68506-0669
402-434-8550

UNITED STATES EQUESTRIAN TEAM
Pottersville Road
Gladstone, NJ 07934
908-234-1251

UNITED STATES PONY CLUB
4071 Iron Works Pike
Lexington, KY 40511
606-254-7669

UNITED STATES TEAM PENNING ASSOCIATION
PO Box 161848
Fort Worth, TX 76161
800-848-3882

WESTERN STOCK SHOW ASSOCIATION
4655 Humboldt Street
Denver, CO 80216-2818
303-297-1166

Glossary

barrel racing: a timed contest in which a mounted rider makes sharp turns around three barrels set in a cloverleaf pattern

bosal: a type of hackamore bridle with a simple noseband made of leather or rope attached to a large knot under the horse's chin

breastplate: also known as a breastband or breast collar; a device used across a horse's chest that attaches to the saddle and prevents it from slipping

bridle: a head harness used to control and guide a horse when driving or riding; consists of a headstall and reins with a bit

bridle path: a section of mane on the top of a horse's head where the mane is trimmed to form a path for the halter or bridle to rest

bit: the mouthpiece on a bridle; there are many different types available

cantle: the rear part of a saddle that projects upward

cinch: *see* girth

crop: a short riding whip with a looped lash

cross-country: a race that includes such events as timed hunter trials and chasing events both of which are ridden at speed over natural fixed fences

crown piece: a piece of the bridle that goes over the horse's head and attaches to the cheekpiece

curb bit: a bit with various mouthpieces and shanks, usually with a center rise that shifts pressure from the tongue to the roof of the mouth

dressage: a form of exhibition riding in which the horse receives nearly invisible cues from the rider and performs a series of difficult steps and gaits with lightness of step and perfect balance. Dressage also is a classical training method that teaches the horse to be responsive, attentive, willing, and relaxed for the purpose of becoming a better equine athlete.

D-ring: a D-shaped metal fitting through which various parts of the harness pass

endurance horse: a horse who competes in endurance competition

farrier: a person who shoes horses

feed: grain used for nourishment

fetlock: a joint that makes a projection on the back of a horse's lower leg above the back of the hoof

frog: the triangular-shaped horny pad near the rear of the sole of a horse's foot

girth: a band that encircles a horse's belly to hold a saddle on the horse's back

gullet: in a western saddle, the open space under the horn

halter: a headpiece of leather, rope, or nylon used to lead a horse

hackamore: a type of bridle with a noseband that applies pressure on the nose for control instead of using a mouthpiece

hand: a standard of equine height measurement derived from the width of a human hand. Each hand equals 4 inches, with fractions expressed in inches. A horse who is 16.2 hands is 16 hands, 2 inches, or 66 inches tall at the withers.

handling: working with a horse while standing on the ground

headstall: the pieces of a bridle including the cheek-strap, throatlatch, browband, and noseband if used

horn: the projection above the raised part in the front of a western saddle

lameness: the condition of having a painful injury of the foot or leg that makes the horse limp or have an irregular gait

lasso: a 30- to 40-foot-long rope with a running noose used for catching horses and cattle

latigo: a strap that secures a girth to a saddle

lead rope: a rope made out of cotton or nylon that can be clipped to a horse's halter

martingale: a device for steadying a horse's head or maintaining proper head carriage

muck heap: a pile located away from the stable where manure and soiled bedding are piled for removal

muck out: to remove manure and soiled bedding from a horse's living area

noseband: part of an English bridle comprising a strap that goes over the nose

open rein: a training action of holding a rein in each hand and directing a turn by holding one rein down toward the rider's knee in the direction of the turn

pastern: part of the back of the foot between the fetlock and hoof

pulling the mane: thinning the hair in the mane by pulling part of the hair out; this can also be done to thin the tail

purebred: a horse of a distinct breed whose parents are registered in the same studbook without mixture of other breeds

rasp: to file down the sharp edges on a horse's teeth

sheath: the organ that encases an unextended penis

show jumping: the competitive riding of horses one at a time over a course of obstacles; horses and riders are judged on ability and speed.

show jumpers: people and horses who compete in show jumping

smegma: the secretion within the sheath of a male horse

snaffle: a type of mild bit

splints: a condition in which a bony growth forms on the cannon bone (lower leg) of a horse; tearing of a ligament between the cannon bone and a neighboring splint bone causes a hot, painful swelling followed by the formation of a splint

split reins: western-style reins that do not join at their ends

tack (tackle): saddle, bridle, and other equipment used in riding and handling a horse

three-day eventer: a horse who competes in a competition that continues over three consecutive days and includes a dressage test, a cross-country event, and show jumping

throatlatch: a bridle strap that goes under the horse's throat

tree (saddletree): the frame of a saddle

withers: the highest part of a horse's back, where the neck and the back join

ABOUT THE AUTHOR

Lesley Ward is the editor of Young Rider *(published by Fancy Publications),*
a magazine dedicated to teaching young people, in an easy-to-read and
entertaining way, how to properly look after their horses and
safely improve their riding skills.

She is also the author of three "how-to" books for children:
The Young Rider's Guide to Buying a Pony,
The Young Rider's Guide to Caring for a Horse or Pony *and*
The Young Rider's Guide to Riding a Horse or Pony.

Lesley enjoys eventing and trail-riding her horse, Murphy, and
teaching children how to ride on her farm in Lexington, KY.

MORE GREAT HORSE TITLES AVAILABLE!

FANCY PUBLICATIONS

Horse Illustrated

The Western Horse

Young Rider

Equine Athlete

Thoroughbred Times

Horses USA

BOWTIE PRESS

Appaloosa Spirit

Arabian Spirit

Paint Spirit

Quarter Horse Spirit

Thoroughbred Spirit

Horses! A Fun & Care Book